**A
LIBRARY PARTNERS PRESS
AWARD WINNER**

David Coates

NON-FICTION AWARD

2020

Advance Praise

In *Historic Houses of Worship in Peril,* Dr. Thomas E. Frank provides a nuanced and compelling argument for the cultural and social value of America's sacred architecture.

Blending historical analysis, detailed case studies from a small New England city, and personal reflection, Frank offers an urgent reminder of why religious congregations and their buildings matter as civic assets apart from their sectarian value —and what is at stake when our society loses them. Though the book convincingly covers the scope of a long-brewing and growing crisis, Frank also points to potential solutions to help save these cultural icons from disappearing from this country's towns and cities.

Throughout the treatise, he both draws and illuminates the disciplines of historic preservation, congregational studies, urban development, and American religious and architectural history to give the reader an insightful and timely treatment on an important and under researched topic.

Tuomi Joshua Forrest, Executive Director, Historic Germantown

In *Historic Houses of Worship in Peril,* Thomas Frank nicely lays out the case for how historic houses of worship serve as community anchors, symbols of neighborhood character, places of personal and collective memory, and sites of cultural identity. In short, they are not just individual landmarks, but, as he describes, "essential elements of the sense of place that grounds community life in America." Unfortunately, as he also describes, social and religious changes over time and across the American civic landscape means that these key community assets are seriously threatened, and too often are disappearing. In summarizing a variety of approaches and scenarios to save these places, Frank makes clear that "driving the collective will to save and use these buildings," must start by by recognizing the broader community values they represent, and which they still advance today.

Paul W. Edmondson, President & CEO, National Trust for Historic Preservation

HISTORIC HOUSES OF WORSHIP IN PERIL

Conserving Their Place in American Life

Thomas Edward Frank
University Professor
Wake Forest University

WIPF & STOCK · Eugene, Oregon

Wipf and Stock Publishers
199 W 8th Ave, Suite 3
Eugene, OR 97401

Historic Houses of Worship in Peril
Conserving Their Place in American Life
By Frank, Thomas Edward
Copyright © 2020 by Frank, Thomas Edward All rights reserved.
Softcover ISBN-13: 979-8-3852-3891-0
Hardcover ISBN-13: 979-8-3852-3892-7
eBook ISBN-13: 979-8-3852-3893-4
Publication date 8/14/2025
Previously published by Library Partners Press, 2020

This edition is a scanned facsimile of the original edition published in 2020.

to Gail

who turned to me in 2006

as we were driving up Main Street

North Adams, Massachusetts

and said why don't you study this

this is perfect

and as always

she was right

TABLE OF CONTENTS

Prelude		vii
Foreword		xv
I.	Introduction	1
II.	Case Studies of Peril and Promise	9
III.	Historic Houses of Worship as Sites of Memory	25
IV.	Historic Houses of Worship as Sites of Ethnic and Cultural Identity	39
V.	The Public Place of Historic Houses of Worship	47
VI.	Houses of Worship as Contested Spaces	65
VII.	Interpreting Religious Architecture and Design	85
VIII.	Scenarios for Historic Houses of Worship	105
Postlude		127
Endnotes by Page Number		131
Appendix: Where to Begin: Resources for Congregations and Communities		141
Acknowledgments		147

Kathedrale (woodcut 1919): © 2020 Artists Rights Society (ARS), New York / VG Bild-Kunst, Bonn

PRELUDE

When I was growing up, my family attended church in a great stone building called Grace Methodist (now United Methodist) Church in St. Louis, Missouri. I was forever in awe of this structure, with its massive red wooden entry doors, soaring fluted plaster arches, and sweeping dark wooden pews seating perhaps 600 or more participants. The curve of the pews directed attention toward a center pulpit, the mirroring curve of choir pews, a 3500-pipe organ chamber, and the ethereal figures of angels depicted in a plaster frieze high above the platform. The late morning light (the 11:00 a.m. service was the one to attend) would sparkle through the brilliant reds and blues of a southerly facing stained glass rose window. Evening services would bring me into the warm yellow hues of afternoon sun glowing through a 30-foot tall Gothic stained glass window of biblical figures in the west wall.

While I had my share of moving experiences in this place, inspired by music or elevated by preaching, my enduring wonder has always been about the building itself. What made it work as a sacred space? Who designed it and with what in mind? What does it mean to the people who come here? Do other people remember this space, the scene of life events and friendships and public rhetoric, as vividly as I do? How does this building frame people's imagination about this community, this city, this land?

The wonder grew toward mystery as I would slip into my secret stairway when few people were around. Sunday afternoon just before youth group was a good time. Almost nobody knew about these hushed stairs; climbing steeply around narrow bends, they took me past the door of the pastor's study and along a passage with an unmarked locked entry to the organ chamber. A jog right and then left connected the passage with what felt almost like a catwalk along the rear of the modernist chapel inserted in this 1913 building in the '50s. Here was another door, sometimes open, leading to steps down into the chapel balcony.

But I would be hard pressed to say whether I preferred those upstairs wanderings to the dank and musty basement. Down some steep cement stairs lighted by a bare bulb, I could find myself in the depths of the boiler room—especially thrilling in winter when the burners would roar to life and the dials on various meters would start to dance. And along the walls in these basement rooms I could find old furniture, light fixtures, files, the detritus of earlier generations that apparently no one had the courage to throw away.

To me, everything in this building of Grace told a story. I didn't know most of these stories, but I knew they were there in the stones, the plaster, the boiler pipes, and even in the cast-offs. The mystery of unknown narratives drew me to their material manifestation like a moth to a flame. I just wanted to be in their presence.

Recently I toured another house of worship with friends and colleagues from Partners for Sacred Places in Philadelphia. I had the privilege of serving for several years as chair of the board of directors of this national non-profit that offers advocacy, training, and resources for historic houses of worship. We were exploring Shiloh Baptist Church, a building designed in 1868 by architects Fraser, Furness, and Hewitt for the Episcopal Church of the Apostles and purchased by the 3000-member Baptist congregation in 1945. Membership was now down to 200 or so, but the building was starting to house vibrant programs in the arts brokered by Partners' initiative on Arts in Sacred Places.

At several points I heard the group calling out my name from a distance. I had wandered off to look at the handsome wooden lockers of the 1900-vintage gym, still standing open as if the athletes had just left. I was spellbound by the elegant glazed ceramic fireplace surround and sliding pocket doors of what had once been a church parlor. I was determined to get a mental map in my head so I could grasp how we got from a third floor assembly room with walls of broken plaster to the creaking balcony looking over a grand nave with 1000 seats. I was trying to understand how this building worked. I was listening for the stories of its rich and complex history.

Today there are many thousands of houses of worship like Shiloh Baptist and Grace Methodist striving to stay open and to serve their communities. Many thousands of other buildings are on the verge of being closed or stand vacant. While a good number have found new uses, many now confront their communities with a troubling issue of blight. Hundreds of cities, towns, and rural crossroads struggle to find any feasible use for these imposing and symbolic structures.

But the issue is greater than blight. Historic houses of worship tell stories of human aspirations and values, of cultural persistence and change, of aesthetic expression and elevation of the human spirit. They are focal points of community narrative, landmarks in neighborhood sense of place. What happens to them is not only—or, for the empty ones, even primarily—a matter of faith or religious practice, whatever form that may take. What becomes of them is inseparable from our sense of awe at how the past is always present: who were the people who built them? To what did they aspire? For what kind of society did they hope? How did they shape what this community has become?

No one really knows how to mitigate this perilous trend of deteriorating houses of worship, and certainly no individual or organization is in a position to address nationally the material problem of what to do with a burgeoning number of empty or underutilized religious buildings. My purpose in this book is to describe the critical and compelling issues at stake for American society and culture, and at the end, point toward promising approaches that town by town, neighborhood by neighborhood, can make a difference. Above all I write to advocate and open a way toward a new imagination for the public role of these significant places.

Many people have commented to me that I must feel nostalgic when I explain my activities in historic preservation, or tell what to me is a compelling story, such as my experience of Grace Church. Indeed, because much of this book examines the past, my passion for conserving historic religious buildings might be facilely dismissed as nostalgia. But this view reflects a profound misunderstanding of the difference between learning how the past has shaped the present and wishing to go back.

Nostalgia is literally homesickness—a longing for home, for places that now are far away or no longer exist. Nostalgia is a kind of dis-ease with the present, with changes from the life of earlier times, a clinging to the "good old days." The fundamental error in nostalgia is three-fold: first, such golden ages never actually existed the way they appear in our elaborated memories; second, images of the remembered past regularly omit constructive changes that have occurred since then, which would mitigate any realistic desire to go back; and third, nostalgia often stirs not only a distaste for the present but disdain for the stranger who represents unwanted change. While it appears passive and sentimental, nostalgia can veil a desire for control of one's self and one's environment. Nostalgia can become an exercise of cultural and social—and in worst cases political—power. When people in any organization start using a fantastical past as a blueprint for restoration, their desires paralyze plans and actions responsive to the current context. When people of a nation start down this path, seeking a return to "homeland," their desires can lead to state control and violence.

Religious leaders tire of parishioners or constituents talking of the good old days. "I remember when"—and fill in the blank here: the youth group had fifty kids, we had to put chairs in the aisle for Easter or Yom Kippur, the kitchen and dining room designed and furnished to serve hundreds of people were filled for congregational dinners every week. Leaders of any organization hear similar reminiscences, but this sentimentality has been rife in houses of worship as so many congregations struggle to stay open. It is easy to dismiss these mental pictures as nostalgia; they fit the three-fold error above. What people remember is not what really happened, nobody really wants to go back to the way families and communities were then, and this kind of talk seems to block all the needed changes.

Leaders need to ask and hear, though, what is really being said behind the words. Most often these memories and descriptions are indirect ways of talking about what people most value about the congregation and community. They are an appeal for the kind of energy and focus that will carry the organization forward, and that will transform the community. This reflects a very different mental framework from the wish to go back.

Remembering stories of the past, asking how buildings came to be, or who the people were who populated this house of worship and this community, or what events occurred that forever shaped the town or the region, are not acts of nostalgia. They are explicitly anti-nostalgic. They express a determined effort to understand how we got to this point, what the motives and aspirations of the people were, how the economy functioned and how society was organized. Understanding the historical dimension reaching across time and space and deepening our perceptions is essential in planning for a constructive future.

The more we can learn about the past, the more we will realize both the good and evil and the mass of gray in between that have brought us the built landscapes and the kinds of communities we have. And from that knowledge we can think more richly and constructively about how to sustain and direct these buildings now toward the aspirations and values, the culture and the sense of place, of today's communities. To do so will require a fresh imagination, and to stir such imaginings is the purpose of this book.

FOREWORD

In the five years since this book was originally published, the issues it addresses have only become more acute. Thousands of houses of worship across the United States, United Kingdom, and Europe are falling empty. Most are Christian church buildings, reflecting a generational change in participation, if not in adherence to, Christian teachings.

Even a cursory look through real estate sites reveals an astonishing number of these buildings being sold by their congregations or denominations. Virtually every community in Western societies is faced with such empty structures. Many churches were constructed with grand conceptions of Christian gathering in worship, their fine architecture joining other monumental buildings in their town or neighborhood—courthouses, public schools, post offices, banks, and fraternal organizations. Once functioning as landmarks of community identity, many now signal abandonment and blight.

Of course, tens of thousands of churches, synagogues, mosques, and other houses of worship continue to thrive. Through worship, education, community service, and public events they strive to be a force for the well-being of their communities. Some congregations and denominations have been able to absorb empty buildings by converting them for use by new congregations or by specialized ministries such as day care or services for unhoused people. Some houses of worship on the market are bought by congregations of other denominations or faiths.

The number of vacant buildings, though, is simply overwhelming in many communities. A decade of declining Mass attendance prompted the Roman Catholic Diocese of Buffalo to close 89 worship sites at once in 2024. On a smaller scale, cities of 10-20,000 may find themselves with half a dozen closed churches right on Main Street or prominent neighborhood corners. Many other churches have an unsustainable mismatch between the size of the structure and the number and resources of participants. Even if a congregation still owns and uses their building, many do not have the funds to maintain it and it steadily deteriorates. It's not only a dismal look for any town, but also a huge challenge to find new purposes for these facilities.

The worsening situation stirred only tepid and scattered interest for decades. Pastors and denominational executives didn't like to discuss it. City government and businesses just shook their heads and figured it was the congregation's problem. Foundations had other priorities. But in recent years as the wave of closures has swelled, so has interest in tackling the problems and possibilities these buildings pose. After all, everyone has a stake in what happens to them—businesses, banks, local governments, social service and non-profit organizations, and neighborhood associations, among many.

To mark its 35th year in 2024, as the only national non-denominational non-profit specifically addressing the revitalization of houses of worship, Partners for Sacred Places hosted a national convening of leaders in business, foundations, denominations, historic preservation, and community organizations. "Activating Hidden Assets: Making the Most of Sacred Places for the Community" was the first of its kind, a gathering that coalesced remarkable energy around working collaboratively to engage the crisis. Together with a new book of essays titled Gone for Good: Negotiating the Coming Wave of Church Property Transition,[1] such resources are sparking widespread interest in new approaches to convert these structures to broader community use. Articles are appearing in publications and social media sites as diverse as the fields of urban planning, public policy, city government, and private enterprise. The need for a coordinated approach by a variety of stakeholders is more apparent than ever.[2]

The last five years have brought encouraging growth in numbers of consultants and advocates for finding new uses for houses of worship. Most are focused, not on converting these structures to private homes or market-rate apartments or condos, but rather on repurposing them for continued community development. Promising approaches now include building affordable housing on church land, incorporating the house of worship; or preserving the worship space for congregations while converting the rest of the property to community service organizations; or adapting spaces for public uses such as music and theater performances, art centers, and museums.

All such approaches, though, require a transformed mindset. As this book explores especially in Chapter VI, viewing these buildings primarily as private property must give way to seeing them as public assets for community use. A more public-facing approach opens the way for a broad range of public and private organizations to help redevelop these spaces to meet community needs. Congregations will find this transformative as well, as they find new partners for sustaining their facilities into the next generation.

One compelling image for a new mindset comes from the passion for creating a strong sense of place in neighborhoods and cities. Common to the fields of architecture, landscape design, urban planning, and community development is a conviction that place-making is one of the key endeavors in nurturing a culture of well-being. As I argue in Chapter V, houses of worship are key historic and visual elements of a sense of place. In terms used by growing numbers of leaders, sacred and civic place-making go hand in hand.

Partnership and collaboration are the keys to unlocking the potential of historic houses of worship. Community organizations, businesses, and local governments need to get to know these buildings and the congregations committed to reenvisioning them. Congregations need to take steps toward civic engagement by finding these new partners and opening new conversations.

This book is a manifesto for collaboration to save these historic buildings, and an invitation to reimagine their purpose and get involved in local community efforts. Whether you are a civic leader, a neighborhood activist, a devoted member of your congregation, or simply someone who loves your community and wants to see it thrive, we all know this:

We must not lose these remarkable sacred—and civic—spaces.

Endnotes

1. Mark Elsdon, Editor. Eerdmans, 2024.

2. See especially articles by Richard T. Reinhard, a consultant with cross-over expertise in both urban planning and religious organizations. "Tsunami of Church Closings Poses Crisis and Opportunity" *Public Square, A Congress for the New Urbanism Journal* (August 13, 2024); "Community Hubs: YIGBY (Yes in God's Backyard) Movement Finds New Uses for Declining Houses of Worship" *Urban Land Magazine* (September 3, 2024); "Get to Know Your City Government: 6 Free Ways to Get Started" *Faith and Leadership* (November 12, 2024); with Thomas Edward Frank, "Church Must Address Property Issues in Net-Zero Effort" *United Methodist News* (September 1, 2021); and a summary of Reinhard's work, "He's Got a Rice Business Degree; now he's focused on finding best use for church buildings" *Baptist News Global* (November 27, 2023).

Photo Captions

(All photos by the author.)

Introduction: Main Street, North Adams, MA, looking eastward toward Monument Square.

Chapter III: Link Auctions, former St. John's United Methodist

Church, St. Louis, MO, north elevation.

Chapter IV: All Saints Episcopal Church (former St. John's Episcopal Church), North Adams, south elevation, with "urban renewal" mall and parking lots in background.

Chapter V: Auditorium, Massachusetts College of Liberal Arts (former Congregation Beth Israel Synagogue), North Adams, MA, west elevation with menorah figure embedded in brick façade.

Chapter VI: Former Roman Catholic church, Blackinton neighborhood, North Adams, MA, renovation for new use paused for lack of funds.

Chapter VII: First Baptist Church, North Adams, MA, south elevation with shadow of the Congregational Church steeple across Main Street.

Chapter VIII: Demolition of former St. Francis of Assisi Roman Catholic Church, North Adams, MA, 2016.

I.
INTRODUCTION

No building type of historical, social, or architectural interest has been more prominent in the built landscape of the United States than churches and synagogues. Houses of worship stand on town squares, intersections of metropolitan arteries, rural hilltops, and freeway interchanges in every region of the country. Church buildings have been thoroughly absorbed into the cultural imagination. Steeples, rooflines, windows, porticoes, and courtyards appear as elements of town logos, symbols of peace and consolation on postcards and greeting cards, notable sites in promotions and tours of historic districts and cultural heritage areas, and settings for family and public events commemorated in photographs, historical booklets, and websites.

Houses of worship are so ubiquitous in North America that one is hard-pressed to notice them, that is, to take note of their significance. They are one of the most taken-for-granted tangible and spatial realities of American society. No one knows how many congregations exist in the United States; a good estimate is between 320,000 and 350,000 including all religious faiths. All share in varying ways in what sociologist of religion Stephen Warner termed "de facto congregationalism." Religious groups of whatever stripe and polity inevitably function as local voluntary associations, governing themselves through boards and councils, and developing varied activities of worship, education, and service. Almost all congregations gather indoors, seeking shelter in a structure. Some move about among homes or rented spaces. But a common mark of generic or "de facto" congregationalism is the aspiration to build, own, and operate a building.

An astonishing number and variety of religious buildings, then, perhaps a quarter million or more, punctuate the American landscape. Their very omnipresence masks critical questions of their purchase on the cultural imagination. These questions are surfacing more urgently because of the emerging crisis of historic religious buildings. Many houses of worship are in peril, their future as intact buildings and sites at risk. Most are over fifty years old and many date from the avid church-building era of 1870 to 1930. Many have survived from the settlement periods of American colonies or in towns and cities of the early 19th century trans-Appalachian West. Thousands of these buildings—perhaps tens of thousands—are occupied by congregations that lack the human or financial resources to maintain or restore their facilities. Many are vacant or listed on the real estate market. Thousands have been rehabilitated for use as commercial or residential space. Untold numbers have already been demolished and are lost forever.

Perhaps the global reach of these trends is some reassurance. England has so many closed or underutilized houses of worship that the National Churches Trust and other agencies have undertaken an actual census of all churches (a project much more feasible on an island than on a continent!) in order to develop a database for tracking their use and condition. National and county organizations such as the Churches Conservation Trust have arisen to help villages, towns, and urban neighborhoods find constructive conversions for vacant spaces. Real estate websites across Europe—from Italy to the Czech Republic to Sweden—are just as abounding in listings for houses of worship, convents, and religious school buildings as US sites are. As in other regions, Australian realtors highlight the eye-popping and upscale renovations that can turn a church into a private residence.

Knowing that we are not alone in our dilemmas over the future of houses of worship perhaps can give us more confidence in addressing the peculiarly American context in which we must act. Historic houses of worship are the built evidence of the settlement of the United States, youngest of the very large nations of the world and thus freshest in telling the story of diverse macro-scale migration across a continent with a relatively small and dispersed aboriginal population before 1600. Churches, synagogues, mosques, and other religious buildings reflect the North American movement and settlement of ethnic and cultural groups from around the world. Historic houses of worship likewise reflect the religious trends and changes that mark 21st century American society. Many continue to house thriving congregations, often making major contributions to the social capital of their communities. Many have been refurbished and continue to extend the religious, ethnic, and cultural traditions they represent into a new millennium.

Many other historic houses of worship, though, belong to diminishing congregations, vivid symbols of how religious affiliation and participation patterns are changing today. These patterns have been studied and analyzed extensively, but no one can predict with certainty how the next decades will unfold. Four markers of these patterns that have been most influential for religious buildings would seem to be these:

- The decline in birthrate among religious adherents of those groups that were the most prolific church-builders of earlier generations, particularly Protestant groups with roots in England and Europe (especially Episcopalians, United Methodists, Presbyterians, Congregationalists, Lutherans, and Baptists). Many researchers argue that as much as 80% of the decline in adherence in these traditions can be attributed to smaller families and fewer children to make up the pool of potential membership. Church buildings constructed before 1960 usually have far more classroom, assembly, and recreational space than a current congregation needs.

- Absorption of immigrant groups into the larger population through intermarriage and cultural change. While "new immigrant" groups conduct worship and education in native tongues (such as Korean or Spanish) and many meet in older religious buildings, immigrant groups of earlier generations no longer seek to maintain ethnic or regional identities through congregational or parish life. This factor accounts for the largest portion of the massive closures of Catholic parish churches across the United States.
- Suburbanization and population shifts. In Chapters Two and Seven I relate the story of congregations in St. Louis, Missouri, continually moving westward over nearly 200 years from the original city center into new urban housing developments and finally to expanding suburbs with a new built landscape and street pattern. In one form or another, this story has been told in every metropolitan region of the U.S. These movements have had numerous effects, among them the dispersal of population cohorts that supported particular congregations, and the sluggishness of established denominational organizations to develop strategies for continuing their presence in older urban neighborhoods while also

expanding their presence in new suburbs. Moreover, much suburban growth is attributable to the influx of population from smaller towns and countryside. Many small towns and rural crossroads have seen their Main Streets and country markets boarded up, with a corresponding loss of adherents in rural and small town churches. A simpler way to put it is that established religious denominations have found that many of their buildings are perfectly sited for the needs of the 19th century, but in just the wrong places to serve mobile 21st century constituencies.

- A fourth marker of the changing landscape for historic houses of worship is the apparent shift in forms of association that characterizes American society. A number of scholars have noted the decline in membership and participation of face-to-face associational life, from civic clubs to fraternal orders to political parties to community organizations. Some studies show that actual attendance in religious services is substantially lower than opinion polls report, especially since the turn of the century. The highly publicized growth of extremely large congregations does not offset the continued shrinkage in participation in congregational life across the religious landscape. While Americans are more networked, linked, and friended than ever through the Internet, what form of embodied association they will seek in the future is unknown. We do not know yet what difference the absorption of people's time into digital media will make to the structure of community life, but religious association stands at the center of this question.

Given these and other markers of change, significant rethinking and reimagining of the place of historic religious buildings in American culture is more pressing with each passing year. While any number of possible strategies are evolving that may help local communities manage and find new uses for these buildings, what is really crucial now is finding a fresh way to understand their place and role in American society and culture. Historic houses of worship have been significant markers in building American communities. The challenge today is to reimagine their place as public spaces and community gathering points for future generations.

In the following chapter I describe the two case studies I have developed in recent years to illustrate and understand more fully the peril of historic houses of worship. In Chapters Three, Four, and Five I explore three dimensions of the place of houses of worship in American culture: religious buildings as sites of memory, as locus of communal pilgrimage and identity, and as critical elements in the sense of place of American communities. In Chapter Six I examine religious buildings as contested spaces, particularly as sites of tension between cultural heritage and the real estate market. In Chapter Seven I interpret historic houses of worship as fluid ventures in architecture and human use. I conclude in Chapter Eight by proposing brief scenarios for the future of historic houses of worship and the implications for American culture that each possibility projects.

This is *not* a book about how to save a church building, where to get funding to assess or replace a slate roof, how to convert a synagogue to a new use, or what a community can do if houses of worship close. Ample resources for these pressing questions can be found through the websites of Partners for Sacred Places, the National Trust for Historic Preservation, or state and local preservation offices and organizations. A basic list of websites and other resources may be found in the Appendix.

This book is intended to help all of us—whether passionate about these buildings or even just curious about them or feeling pressed to do something about them—to reconsider some of our assumptions about them, to learn more deeply about their meaning to those who experience them, and to perceive more clearly their place in society and culture. If this book stirs readers to take action, that would be terrific. If this book inspires a new paradigm for thinking about historic houses of worship, that would be even better. Only then can a national cultural movement coalesce around possibilities of a thriving future for these structures of transcendent beauty and profound significance.

II.
CASE STUDIES OF PERIL AND PROMISE

I conduct this exploration through case studies of the fate of religious buildings in North America—cases that could be multiplied many times over in settlements across the land. Here are two that offer distinct stories, contexts, and perspectives on the peril and promise of historic houses of worship.

1. North Adams, Massachusetts

"North Adams has traveled the long road back from dying mill town to one of the region's significant cultural destinations." Appalachian Trail Journeys, 2008

"Set against a New England backdrop of buxom hills flecked with steeples, [the Massachusetts Museum of Contemporary Art has] an undeniable charm." Escapes section, New York Times, 2008

"North Adams has a decidedly more hip and edgy vibe than the rest of the Berkshires, much of which is

known for sprawling vacation homes, 19th century estates and cultural offerings like Tanglewood. Here's an inside look at what makes North Adams the Hamptons of the New England area." CNN Travel (06/24/2019) https://www.cnn.com/travel/article/north-adams-massachusetts-tourists/index.html

The case to which I refer most frequently is the city of North Adams, Massachusetts. This is the lesser known old industrial town adjacent to the much more publicized Williamstown that tags itself "The Village Beautiful"—home of Williams College, the Broadway warm-up summer stage of the Williamstown Theater Festival, the Clark Art Institute, and dozens of elegant second homes and developments.

As I drive west on Route 2 in western Massachusetts—a road marketed since early in the automobile era as the Mohawk Trail—I wend my way up the Deerfield River into the wooded hills above Charlemont. The road then climbs with the Cold River higher up into the Berkshire towns of Savoy and the unlikely-named Florida (founded the year Florida became a state). At last I reach an outlook from the Western Summit. If I pull across into the parking area, I will have a first grand vista across the Hoosic River Valley and the city of North Adams. The view becomes more vivid as I descend a steep grade into a curve known to generations of tourists as the Hairpin Turn, and a realization dawns that the most prominent architectural feature of the city skyline is the steeples of its churches.

By the time I have dropped rapidly down the hills into town, arrived on Center Street, and turn over to Main, the steeples are towering 150 feet over my head. No other building in North Adams, even with the city's history of bustling industries and commerce, reaches that height. No less than four houses of worship with tall spires stand within a block of Monument Square at the city center.

North Adams is best known in recent years as the home of the Massachusetts Museum of Contemporary Art—recognized by its brand logo MASS MoCA. The story of the museum is often cited as an exemplar of the potential of the "creative economy" to remake older American industrial settlements by infusing old mill and factory buildings with a new generation of artists, craftspeople, and designers. MASS MoCA is only one initiative among several efforts in North Adams to rehabilitate vacant mill buildings into live/work lofts for creative work. Several hundred new residents have moved to town to practice their crafts and many small galleries have sprung up in vacant storefronts of the 19th century streetscape.

Yet strikingly enough, the city of North Adams continues to view its monumental houses of worship as its distinct signature. The town branding slogan is "City of Steeples," the baseball team in the summer collegiate league is named the SteepleCats, and the mall near the town center is the Steeple City Plaza. Joe Manning, an independent writer who conducted extensive interviews of residents and has published two books on the history and changes of North Adams that include many historic and contemporary skyline photographs, has catalyzed this slogan in part with his book entitled *Steeples: Sketches of North Adams*.

Indeed the city's church steeples are unquestionably its most prominent landmarks. The four houses of worship with steeples—Baptist, Congregational, Episcopal, and (former) Roman Catholic—are joined by four other substantial religious buildings with lower towers, including a (former) United Methodist Church now renovated into an art gallery, the consolidated Roman Catholic parish, a (former) synagogue now a college auditorium, and the (former) Universalist (later Unitarian Universalist) Church now an art gallery. These eight historic houses of worship are all within six blocks of each other. Only four are in active use by a congregation. Four are either vacant or have been kept intact while converted to other uses. A fifth steepled church (former Roman Catholic) was demolished in 2016. It's hard to imagine North Adams without these landmarks. Together with the massive 19th century mill buildings, the Hoosac Tunnel that in a remarkable engineering feat brought the railroad through the mountains from Boston, and the graceful forested peaks that surround the valley, the churches are an irreplaceable feature of the city's landscape.

North Adams is a microcosm of American religious history and its material expression in buildings. How a city of 13,000 residents came to have such a built religious landscape is a rich and complex story of economic development, immigration, civic improvement, and cultural aspiration. Its houses of worship exemplify the multiple layers of memory and imagination that cluster around religious buildings and their surroundings.

But what should happen now to historic religious buildings like these? North Adams offers a window into questions that shake many communities around the U.S.—and other nations as well. Whose problem is it when congregations can no longer support such aging landmarks? Does responsibility lie with the congregation or denomination? What role does the neighborhood, town, or city have in saving and finding living uses for such a distinctive element of the local landscape?

2. Holy Corners, St. Louis, Missouri

"Interfaith Event of Holy Corners Set for Tuesday, The twenty-fourth annual fellowship dinner . . ."
St. Louis Post-Dispatch (January 16, 1954) 5.

The saga of Holy Corners at the intersection of Kingshighway Boulevard and Washington Place in St. Louis illustrates how urban religious buildings tell the story of city expansion. In the case of the old river city of St. Louis, it is a story of migration of European-Americans westward from the banks of the Mississippi River. St. John's United Methodist Church, for example, was formed from an earlier congregation dating back to the early 1800s, occupying a building within a few blocks of the Mississippi riverfront at 4th Street. Following the Civil War,

4th Street was becoming the axis of the growing business district and the congregation was dwindling. Uniting with another congregation then located at 24th Street in 1869, the newly named St. John's congregation then erected a fine structure in a new residential area called Stoddard Addition, at Locust and Ewing (today named T. E. Huntley Avenue, what would correspond to 29th Street). This house of worship reflected the growing prosperity of the congregation and city, blending Gothic and Italianate styles in brick, white stone trim, and a campanile tower. All three of these earlier buildings have long since been demolished, though the last was sold to the Roman Catholic diocese in 1902 and renamed St. Charles Borromeo. It served the increasingly Italian immigrant neighborhood, and then as the Italians moved to the suburbs the parish served the incoming African American populace, until it closed and was torn down over widespread public protest in 1989.

In 1900 the St. John's congregation began to look west again, toward new housing developments springing up around the city's magnificent 1400-acre Forest Park. The park had opened in 1876 and was preparing to host the 1904 St. Louis World's Fair. The congregation chose a lot on Kingshighway Boulevard, the major north-south arterial road that forms the eastern boundary of Forest Park. At the corner of Washington Place, about six blocks north of the park, St. John's was the first of a growing configuration of high-style buildings in the neighborhood, including three other houses of worship—First Church of Christ Scientist, Second Baptist Church, and Temple Israel—a Masonic temple, and the Racquet Club. The intersection soon acquired the nickname "Holy Corners."

The prosperous congregation of St. John's (then called St. John's Methodist Episcopal Church, South), described in a local magazine in 1882 as "one of the largest, wealthiest and most influential churches in the city," looked for a prominent architect for their new structure. They selected Theodore C. Link, a local architect best known for his design of the monumental St. Louis Union Station which opened in 1894. One of Link's signature design elements was the use of barrel vaulting to create broad expanses of space without support columns. The Grand Hall of Union Station was so designed, with a 65-foot ceiling and elegant gold leaf and stenciled decorative detail. Not surprisingly, the new St. John's auditorium was constructed with a stunning barrel vaulted ceiling, this time with rows of coffers to give the space even more depth.

While he designed Union Station with Romanesque and Norman elements, including stone cladding, turrets and towers, Link chose a more neo-classical if eclectic style for St. John's. He placed pedimented porticoes with six Ionic columns on both the Washington Street and the Kingshighway elevations, the former sheltering the entrance to the main auditorium wing and the latter entry to the education and fellowship wing. In the right angle formed by the two wings he placed an attached campanile tower to tie the structure into a coherent mass. The entire building was sheathed in cut limestone, including side elevations that are often left in brick by lesser endowed congregations.

Within a few years of its completion in 1902, St. John's found itself anchoring a whole district of houses of worship. Each new building was constructed for congregations that were following the westward migration of the city population from a first generation location near the river, to a second generation site near the previous site of St. John's on streets about thirty blocks west of the river, and finally now looking for a place to build near Forest Park.

In 1907 St. John's was joined directly across Kingshighway by a congregation that had shared much the same history. This was to be the fourth location of Second Baptist Church in St. Louis; their successive addresses along Locust Street, at its intersections with Third Street, Sixth Street, Beaumont (the equivalent of 27th Street), and then Kingshighway, marked the westward progression of the city, and all four of those earlier sites were within two blocks of St. John's and its predecessor congregations at Fourth, Ewing (29th Street), and then Kingshighway. All of these earlier buildings were eventually demolished for commercial development. Only the Kingshighway structures remain.

Second Baptist moved into an elegant high-style Northern Italian Gothic structure comprising over one million bricks of varied hues together with terra cotta and limestone features, making it one of the finest examples of masonry in the region. Designed by the local St. Louis firm of Mauran, Russell and Garden, the new church was centered by a campanile, in this case set in a wide courtyard framed by the U-shape of enfolding wings.

Finally, in 1908 the Temple Israel congregation joined the Holy Corners collection. Founded in 1886 as a Reform synagogue with progressive views, Temple Israel erected its first house of worship near St. John's and Second Baptist at 28th Street. Following the westward flow of its members, the congregation decided to relocate to a third corner of Kingshighway and Washington Place. Their new synagogue was designed in Roman Temple style including a massive columned portico facing the main St. John's columned portico directly across Washington Place. Local architect Tom Barnett also included elegant stone and terrazzo interiors in both the auditorium and the matching education wing.

The three houses of worship at Kingshighway and Washington Place immediately became city landmarks along the north-south thoroughfare. Together the neighboring buildings facing Kingshighway— First Church of Christ, Scientist (1903), constructed in dark brick with classical and Italian Renaissance motifs complete with a columned portico; the imposing five-story earth brown brick Racquet Club (1906); and the classical Tuscan Temple (1908), dark red brick with white columns—as well as First Unitarian Church (now Unitarian Universalist) (1917), a Gothic stone structure on Waterman Boulevard just off Kingshighway—all within a three-block radius—made Holy Corners one of the most prominent intersections in St. Louis. Gated streets in the neighborhood with impressive names like Westminster Place, Portland Place, and Westmoreland Place, enclosed entire blocks of mansions being built during the period. Wealthy "white" Protestant parishioners, among St. Louis's most influential citizens, were delivered by chauffeured cars to the church doors of St. John's on one side of the boulevard and to Second Baptist on the other. They were joined by members who came by trolley on the north-south Euclid Avenue line or the east-west Delmar Boulevard line, both just a block away, congregants arriving from around the city to what had become a worship destination.

Holy Corners had a great run for nearly three generations. But urban dynamics changed dramatically after World War II. The City of St. Louis bought enthusiastically into the urban renewal mentality of the 1950s, with federal funding readily available to encourage mass demolitions as cities strove to shed their deteriorating 19th century streetscapes. An entire swath of riverfront was scraped clean in anticipation of redevelopment, which over a period of forty years finally produced the iconic Gateway Arch National Park, a chain of plazas flowing west, two baseball stadiums in succession, and numerous office buildings and hotels. The neighborhoods immediately west of downtown, including thousands of residences, hundreds of businesses and institutions, and over forty houses of worship in the area earlier vacated by Temple Israel, Second Baptist, and St. John's, had become considerably poorer since "white" people left. Absentee landlords exploited a growing African-American population in need of housing; fine brick townhouses and commercial buildings were deteriorating rapidly. Soon the entire area, including its monumental buildings such as houses of worship, was razed for a promised development of commerce and housing that took decades to materialize. This devastation, leaving parts of St. Louis looking like a ruined meadow, as in many cities, awakened citizens to the potential loss of more historic treasures and their invaluable functional spaces. Ordinances to protect landmarks and districts were soon adopted.

Meanwhile, back at Holy Corners, urban change was producing a sense of failure and decline among "white" constituents. The congregation of Second Baptist saw the trends first, and moved in 1958 to a new facility seven miles farther west on a prosperous suburban artery, Clayton Road. This fifth location in its history was for the first time outside the city limits.

The congregation of Temple Israel was not far behind in westward migration out of the city. Anticipating a long-term boom in suburban housing, the congregation bought a lot four miles farther west of the relocated Second Baptist on a parallel arterial street, Ladue Road. Their move was delayed by the effort of municipalities to block construction of houses of worship through zoning regulations. When the Missouri Supreme Court finally overturned these ordinances, Temple Israel built a new mid-century modernist facility. The congregation carried its Torah scrolls and pulpit Bible out of the 1908 Temple at Holy Corners and processed westward to the new location in August 1962.

Both Second Baptist and Temple Israel were able to sell their facilities at Holy Corners, though with difficulty. The Temple school was purchased by the St. Louis Board of Education in 1966 and used for special education programs for many years. The house of worship itself did not sell for another ten years, and then for only $33,000, to an African-American Pentecostal congregation named Angelic Temple of Deliverance. Second Baptist sold to a congregation named Church of the Good Shepherd, which was followed by other congregations occupying the facility. In each case, the purchasing congregation lacked the financial resources even to replace broken windows, much less to install new roofs, replace heating systems, or similar capital projects.

St. John's Methodist Church remained as a remnant of a Holy Corners now increasingly becoming a shadow of itself. The dominant-culture "white" network of social and religious relationships among the rabbis, pastors, and laity of the three congregations had spawned citywide programs for Jewish-Christian dialogue, an annual fellowship dinner for all faiths, and much of the impetus for the nationally recognized Metropolitan Church Federation of St. Louis. The rabbi and pastors were major figures in the city and the nation. But none of the clergy and perhaps a handful of members were African-American in an area of the city rapidly being evacuated by "whites." All the chemistry of an older social order was dissolving quickly with suburbanization and a new generation of leaders. The east-west Delmar Boulevard that ran just half a block behind Temple Israel was becoming the border between a growing African-American population seeking new housing in neighborhoods north of it and a much wealthier "white" populace south of it seeing itself as increasingly embattled. In fact, of course, the sharp division along Delmar Boulevard was a deliberate real estate and zoning strategy to keep the "races" separate. Many commercial structures, storefronts, and residential buildings along Delmar as well as on Kingshighway north of Delmar were demolished after the 1960s, vastly reducing the population density and the livability of the neighborhood. But St. John's, even after buying a suburban lot for possible relocation, decided to stay.

The congregation lived off a generous endowment for many years, supporting paid professional singers and an organist even when the worshipping congregation dipped below a hundred. Ghosts of the past still hovered in the grand room, in the names on memorial windows, on plaques dedicated to earlier leaders, and in the handsomely lettered seating chart that dated to the days of pew rents (generally frowned on in Methodism) that had hung on the back wall behind the pews since the 1920s. But the dwindling constituents could not keep up with the building.

A facility erected for hundreds of participants and dozens of activities was falling empty. Many rooms simply accumulated junk; walls damaged from roof leaks remained swollen and unpainted; mold was gathering in the basement.

Beginning in 1996, St. John's began an all-out effort to find new ways to use the facilities. Within a few years, a second congregation had begun worshipping in the auditorium; three theater groups were using the full-size gymnasium and stage; and a variety of social and religious non-profit agencies were renting office and activity space. This strategy sustained the building for a decade, and the congregation was able to celebrate its 100th anniversary of presence at Holy Corners in 2003. But by the summer of 2007 the endowment and other financial and human resources were exhausted or diminished to the point of no return. The congregation held its final worship service and was formally discontinued.

Thus ended a century of the continuous presence of well-heeled and prominent congregations at the corner of Kingshighway and Washington Place. Their designer buildings remain, as do persistent questions. Since all the previous buildings of these congregations were demolished, why protect these from demolition? Is the troubled history of the "white" power structure, social class differences, and racial dynamics embodied in these structures really worth preserving, and for whom? And who needs 40,000 square foot buildings with elegant masonry, plaster, and glass that are works of art but expensive to maintain? The Holy Corners Historic District was nominated for the National Register of Historic Places in 1975. Holy Corners is also today a City of St. Louis Landmark and part of the Central West End Historic District of St. Louis, thus protected from demolition or any future alteration incompatible with the original buildings. But preservation does not work without owners who are willing to invest what is needed to save the building. And who might they be?

III.
HISTORIC HOUSES OF WORSHIP AS SITES OF MEMORY

> *"This unique property consisting of a 3800 sq. ft. church plus a 12 room 3600 sq. ft. home awaits your ideas for a new use."* (Real estate flyer, Hinsdale, New Hampshire)

Houses of worship over time and the passage of generations become sites of memory for members and constituents of their congregations, for people who have occasionally attended events there, and for the public who may know the building only as a visual marker of the built landscape. Many participants and observers develop a fierce and lasting attachment to these places, much like my abiding memories of Grace Church, St. Louis. While many other kinds of historic buildings such as county courthouses, public schools, Masonic halls, or railroad stations also face threats of demolition and loss, houses of worship often draw a particular and distinct public attention and sentiment.

As French historian Pierre Nora has argued, sites of memory (*lieux de mémoire*) are sites in three senses: *material*, *symbolic*, and *functional*. Certainly buildings are, first, a *material*, physical presence. Their shape, height, and mass, in relationship with surrounding buildings, become part of the remembered visual landscape of a street. The materials with which they are constructed and decorated, often taken from nearby quarries, clay pits, and forests, recall the composition of the natural terrain.

Many make a prominent statement with the sheer physicality of their presence in the land. Their scale, design, building materials, and siting declare that "we are here"—"we" have a place on the street. This is for some congregations the most public declaration they ordinarily make. By erecting a building that cannot be missed, they claim their place in the community.

Five prominent downtown houses of worship in North Adams, for example, were erected in the period between 1865 and 1888, and one additional building of that period (the Methodist Episcopal Church) stood for over fifty years before burning down in 1927. All six of these original 19th century structures sported steeples of 150 feet or more, in keeping with the widespread presupposition that "a spire was requisite for all church buildings." The structures were designed by architects, not by local builders (the common practice in earlier decades), though several of them were modeled on published building plans for churches of a grand scale. They were constructed with stone foundations and brick walls, with slate or tile roofs. Their architects were drawn to an ideal of the Medieval as the archetype of Christian society, and chose either the elevated spirit of Gothic style or the more fortress-like stolidity of the Romanesque—either was then in fashion as a form for expressing the permanence and centrality of houses of worship. First Congregational Church, for example, adopted a fine Romanesque aesthetic for window and door framing and surrounding masonry, crowned by an extraordinarily tall spire rising from a square base. This design closely followed the popular *Book of Plans for Churches and Parsonages* published by the Congregational Church denomination in 1853. Thus the North Adams church bears much resemblance to other Congregational churches of the period in Massachusetts, New York, and other regions.

The prominence of these houses of worship in the built landscape can be kept in perspective by remembering that they were erected before the skyscraper or high-rise era. At the time North Adams had few buildings of any type more than three stories in height. Their significance was further enhanced by the installation of one or more Tiffany or other high design stained glass windows; top-of-the-line pipe organs such as Moeller and Aeolian-Skinner; and elegantly crafted stone, wood, and plaster in arches, trim features, and altar furnishings. Other than the one destroyed by fire in the 1920s and another recently demolished, all of these center city buildings built in the sixty years between 1870 and 1930 remain largely intact today with few changes in their naves other than minor renovations or added (or removed) decor such as stained glass windows.

The grandeur and stability of these houses of worship, now around 150 years old, is remarkable. Each has made a firm proclamation that the congregation has a place in the land. I have often heard comments about such buildings that their ostentatious design and decoration mark the dominance of the rich in North America. To be sure, their construction would not have been possible without the fortunes earned from new industries and technologies of the 19th century. The middle-class congregations that occupy them today bear the burden of buildings that may have been overbuilt for the size of the worshipping congregation and excessively decorated even for the time. In that sense the materiality of these structures could be associated with the growing prosperity and consumerism of 19th century American culture that only accelerated in the 20th.

But clearly this is not how their contemporaries viewed them. The remarks of The Reverend Thomas Griffin at the opening of the fine Gothic-style Methodist Episcopal Church in 1873 were most revealing in this regard. "We rejoice that our mission has been to the poor," declared Griffin.

> It has been the great glory of our denomination, that while few 'mighty' or wealthy men have, as such, entered her communion, she has lifted thousands of the sons and daughters of penury

to affluence and social position . . . This great commission to 'preach the gospel to the poor,' is held in mind by the projectors of our future temple [the new church]. Its commodiousness insures the fulfillment of the Lord's avowal. 'The poor have the gospel preached unto them,' and though we anticipate an advance in architectural grace . . . we look for the abiding of that spirit of humility and power, which has hitherto been the secret of our success.

Religious buildings of this type were for everyone, in other words (everyone of European ethnicity, that is). They were built for everyday people, declaring and securing materially the place in society of anyone who attended there. Such fine houses of worship required the resources of the rich; the Methodists had relied for two-thirds of their building costs on local industrialist Harvey Arnold (owner of Arnold Print Works, the building complex now occupied by MASS MoCA). Nonetheless, such grand churches physically embodied the open access to land, materials, and opportunity for expression so essential to Americans' understanding of democratic society.

That religious buildings become, secondly, *symbolic* sites seems almost a truism. But they are symbolic not only because, in their shape and decoration, they incorporate depictions, signs, or expressions of the faith tradition in which they were built. Their symbolic presence widens and deepens through their use over time. It is generated by the flows of people whose feet have worn away the surface of the granite steps; by rituals marking the life passages of birth, marriage, or death in a sacred space; by the interaction of people of multiple generations and backgrounds who make a life in a place together. A building that has endured for generations and resonates with the voices of children, with footsteps of people seeking food, shelter, or companionship, with banter and discussion and forceful speech that marks public meetings, comes to represent essential elements and practices of communal and public life.

The "symbolic resonance" (to adopt Richard Kieckhefer's fertile term) of houses of worship is embedded in specific spaces and objects. A few years before it was closed, the St. Francis of Assisi Roman Catholic parish council moved a Pieta statue from a small chapel near a side door to a new position against the wall of the nave. A long-time parishioner pointed out to me one Sunday how the hands of the Christ-figure were darker and shinier than the rest of the sculpture. The nuns, he said, would walk from their convent across the intersection through the side door into the sanctuary, touching the wounds of the crucified Christ as they passed by. The oil of their fingers had gradually darkened the stone.

The symbolic resonance of houses of worship also echoes well beyond their interior spaces, beyond even stately architecture or grand building materials. People often care about religious buildings whether or not they have any specific memories of events within them, perhaps because they associate them with something transcendent or lasting—values that sustain a good society, or ritual markers that give meaning and order to the human life cycle.

Religion in whatever form, after all, is at heart a practice of memory. The sacred texts read from bimahs, lecterns, or pulpits; the hymns, responses, and anthems sung by cantors, choirs, and congregations; the rituals enacted from books of prayer or bodily repetition; all are acts through which the participants gathered as a community of memory link themselves to an inheritance. "Religion as a chain of memory," to adopt Danièle Hervieu-Léger's metaphor, binds participants to a living past that is often most vividly embodied in a physical structure that itself enfolds a cluster of memories.

Some of these memories are individual as participants reflect on moments of particular poignancy in their own lives (their wedding ceremony, a speaker that deeply moved them, a hymn they learned from their grandmother). Some are congregational as the gathered community experiences vibrancy (the period when many new families were joining, the priest so much beloved, the glorious renovation of the sanctuary) or passes through hardships (the fire in the organ chamber, the departure of active members, the death of a long-time pastor). Some memories are inseparable from the history of the town, neighborhood, and larger society (World War II when many men were gone or lost to the congregation, the devastation of industries moving away, the growing poverty of many residents). And pervading all the others are the practices that express the faith, worldview, and apprehension of the Holy across many generations.

Vacant houses of worship shake this symbolic resonance to the core. Haunted by the absence of their loyal inhabitants, they manifest the fragmented and broken chains of memory in contemporary society. "The collective memory of modern societies is composed of bits and pieces," Hervieu-Léger argued, a bricolage of symbols collected from "the vast incoherent mass of information" at one's fingertips in "image-fed societies." To the extent that they were once able to "project a lineage of belief" for their constituents, empty religious buildings now represent "the disintegration of the imagined continuity" essential to faith and practice.

The old Notre Dame de Sacre Coeur Roman Catholic building in North Adams has drawn me back several times. It remains vacant after more than a decade on the real estate market, with plastic inserts where stained glass windows used to glow, all interior décor and objects of religious significance removed, and even the cross taken down from the steeple (at a cost to the diocese, I was told, of $5,000 to hire a crane). A strict interpretation of Catholic canon law requires such removals, but vastly diminishes the character and thus the value of such a building. Canon law even makes a valiant effort to shelter traditions and doctrines; a former church is not to be used for purposes incompatible with church teachings (no abortion clinics, for example). So the bishop puts deed restrictions in the sale. But how much force such restrictions can have over a succession of owners is unknown. "It's just sad," said a very somber city official with whom I visited about Notre Dame. "When I think of the weddings and events I attended there . . . I just can hardly stand to look at the building."

The *functions* of religious buildings, their third dimension as sites of memory, may appear to be static because their steeples, sanctuaries, and siting usually well above street level give the sensation of stolid permanence. To the extent that ritual and service activities are passed along from generation to generation and those practices become more or less known in the wider community, people may assume that they know how a building is being used. More broadly, many people simply categorize such buildings as sacred spaces—sacredness often being attributed to houses of worship even by those who do not share the religion practiced there. This assumption connects deeply to religious tolerance, that is, the outlook that each faith can be left to its own way of pursuing the sacred as long as it does not bother other people. Consequently non-participants may be hesitant or even fearful of entering the space of a congregation different from their own, preferring to veil their sketchy sense of "what goes on in there" by naming the building as "sacred."

The problem with mere tolerance, though, (we'll stay out of your business if you stay out of ours) is that it masks dominant cultural markers for what is acceptable. Repeatedly in American history—from the Shakers to the Mormons to Roman Catholicism to Islam—"white" Protestant culture has asserted its dominance through discrimination and occasionally violence. Tolerance has shown its underside of intolerance for any variation from taken-for-granted norms. For the 19th century Protestants of North Adams, the influx of immigrant labor from predominantly Roman Catholic countries in Europe was a cultural challenge. But at least these newcomers built houses of worship that looked like churches and therefore could be assumed to be practicing something familiarly religious. The Methodists even sold their former meeting house on Center Street to the Irish immigrants for their first Masses until they could build St. Francis, whereupon the French immigrants occupied the building until they could construct Notre Dame. The religious mix of North Adams was changing.

Fundamentally static cultural views and assumptions often completely miss what is actually happening in houses of worship as generations roll by. Functions in these buildings have changed continuously over time as new practices evolve and older ones fade from the scene. From the day a building is completed and open for occupancy, its design may or may not accord with its actual use. Houses of worship may be used more intensively in some periods than in others. Their rooms may be altered to accommodate new activities. Their space and style may become increasingly dysfunctional as needs and desires change.

Indeed in recent years the churches of North Adams have already been making numerous adaptations of their physical structures. Before they closed their 1929 building and moved, the United Methodists rarely worshipped in the grand nave since running the heat for a single Sunday could cost $1000. They met in a gathering hall outside the sanctuary, and leased parts of the building to agencies outside the congregation. Similarly, the Congregationalists have been using their historic worship space very seldom and leased out an office and classroom wing the congregation had built in the 1960s along a side street, eventually trying to sell that addition. Meanwhile, the Baptists have modified their auditorium, designed to focus sensory attention on the pipe organ, choir, and pulpit, to incorporate contemporary appeal to the senses through digital technology, with recorded music and visual images emitting from newly installed equipment on the platform. They are attracting relatively large congregations to the historic space.

Inhabitants who are not participants in these congregations know little of how the buildings are actually functioning, although the town rumor mill often passes along gossip about a congregation's struggles to maintain its structure. And if a nonmember attends a concert, lecture, or other public gathering, or comes inside for a community meal or to go to the voting booth, that person would not necessarily know anything about what goes on with church programs.

Yet no attentive inhabitant can miss the change when the church sign is replaced with the name of an art gallery, or when roof tiles are visibly damaged or falling, or when few cars are seen along the streets by the church on a Sunday morning. A sense of decline and loss can spread like a fog across such a small city, blending with the haze of derelict or condemned houses, empty commercial buildings, and a dearth of new construction.

Nora raises the critical question of whether sites of memory, under the pressure of modernism, global capitalism, and social mobility, have morphed into mere form without content: representations of continuity with a past that is no longer accessible except as nostalgic artifact. The *milieux de mémoire* in which a building made sense, embedded in the daily life of a living community, has dissipated under conditions of modernity. As communities have changed, their networks of daily relationships stretched and their continuities of practice pulled apart, so has the symbolic place of the physical structures that represented a shared heritage. This leaves historic sites, Nora argues, to become parodies of themselves; the people who observe them have little organic connection with them or continuity of shared memory with the people who created them.

Indeed, when a neo-Gothic house of worship like the United Methodist Church of North Adams with a sanctuary seating 600 people crossed into the new millenium hosting a regular worshipping congregation of 30, with dozens of activity rooms in the education wing and undercroft closed and unheated, one had to wonder if the practices that generated the physical structure were in any way sufficient to sustain it as a living site. The remnant of this congregation finally had to face giving up any functions in the building and voted to sell and relocate. They were forced to surrender the primary symbolic focus for Methodists in continuous gathering in North Adams for 175 years to a sale of the property on the real estate market. As the congregation took away its individual and collective memories of the building, and their house of worship was modified into a gallery for the arts, in what ways does this site now function as a *lieu de mémoire* for the community?

IV.
HISTORIC HOUSES OF WORSHIP AS SITES OF ETHNIC AND CULTURAL IDENTITY

"Unique and rare opportunity! Two story building currently being used as a church . . . Many possibilities!" (Real estate flyer, Saugus, Massachusetts)

Many houses of worship were built for new immigrant populations of the 19th century. These buildings today present a physical record of the pilgrimage of peoples from homelands around the world to the new land of the United States. Many bear in their names a resonance with the language, culture, and heritage of the people who originally built them. They were sites for the remembering and continuing of a home culture, sustained through festivals, rites, clothing, language, food, and family.

As immigrant communities have dispersed across the land and general population, the use of their historic houses of worship by succeeding generations has become a paramount issue. Many such buildings have been sold to other religious groups. Many are occupied by remnants of the original community. Many are closed or have been adapted for other uses.

The range of houses of worship in North Adams is a vivid cross-section of 19th century immigration. North Adams was a major industrial city with factories making printed cloth, shoes, and electrical parts, located in a pivotal spot at the west end of the Hoosac Tunnel on the railroad from Boston to Albany and westward. The churches represented French Canadian, Irish, Italian, Polish, and Anglo populations, including entire village populations that migrated across the Atlantic to work in the mills. Roman Catholic "national" parishes sprang up one after another, reflecting successive waves of laborers. No sooner had St. Francis of Assisi's house of worship been erected and begun serving mainly the Irish immigrant population in 1869, than the French-speaking parish of Notre Dame du Sacre Coeur was organized, completing its equally fine house of worship in French High Gothic style in 1888. A few years later, the Italians built their own parish church of St. Anthony of Padua, subsequently replacing it with an Art Deco modernist structure in 1958.

These church buildings embodied an aspiration to house and shelter the continuing culture of the people who worshipped there. In language and décor, in festivals and folkways, they offered participants a continuing connection with their homelands. As one Catholic resident told oral historian Michael Hoberman in 2001,

> your social network was all church-related, and so you went there for all of your sustenance, whether it was religious, spiritual, cultural or social . . . it was like you didn't feel like you were going to church if you went to another church other than your own church. And that was really part of that old culture thing from the Old Country.

"National" parishes were not parishes in the historic sense, then—*paroikia* or the area beside or contiguous to (*para-*) the house (*oikos*) of worship. "Parishioners" of the national churches actually overlapped each other in the neighborhoods and crossed paths going to their own buildings.

The long-time director of a local non-profit social service agency, a Jew active in a synagogue in another town, remembered the churches being the basis of community. He "identified kids by which church or synagogue they came from," and everybody talked about how the churches "were competitive with each other" through sports. A Catholic lay woman recalled a bishop in the 1980s trying to convert the parishes from "national" or ethnic to geographic. She and her husband had been attending Notre Dame because it was closest to them, but quickly moved their registration to St. Francis so they would not be forced to register—and thus be identified with—the French parish. The intensity of loyalty to these parishes continues today. Before St. Francis was closed, a couple in their 30s told me after Mass that they had had to go to another town to get married; her family was from the recently closed Notre Dame, and her parents were not about to see their daughter get married in the Italian or Irish parish of North Adams.

The immigrant experience in North America has been much explored around the theme of conflicted identity—how cultural identity was preserved or integrated with other cultures in North America, how it was passed from the first generation to the second to the third (or not), and how identities are constructed and reconstructed, patched and quilted together into complex hybrids. The built landscape of religion has embodied this identity struggle as houses of worship were erected for each ethnic or cultural group. The buildings were a physical announcement of presence in the larger community, marking a stake in the land and a place in the emerging streetscape of a neighborhood. They also served to manage conflict between ethnic groups by allowing them to remain in separate domains. (Of course, as numerous informants have told me, the conflict was also perfectly sublimated for men through the church basketball league; even if fisticuffs broke out, they could be blamed on jockeying for position under the basket instead of ethnic jealousy or hostility.)

Yet the buildings themselves housed multiple claims in tension with each other. An immigrant congregation was inevitably double-minded, as if they were saying, "We are here in America to stay, while we also have constructed a place that shelters and preserves our cultural homeland;" or, "We belong to this community as a distinct immigrant group bearing language and customs from elsewhere, while we also have erected a landmark building to indicate our desire to stay and participate in this society." So the parishes bore a dual purpose: on one side as havens for immigrants with a common heritage and shelters for the continuity of language and culture; and on the other as place holders for enabling their participants to enter into the life of the larger community. They were stewards of what French sociologist Maurice Halbwachs termed the "collective memory" of their constituents grounded in stories of their heritage and homeland. At the same time, they were enablers of a broader collective memory being created by the collision and collaboration of many different ethnic heritages in the formation of the society and culture of the town.

The question then becomes whether today's participants can or should draw on communal ethnic heritage for their faith practices. Clearly, while much religious participation in North America, and certainly in North Adams, has been ascriptive—a world into which one is simply born and socialized by virtue of family and ethnic ties—participation has largely gravitated toward American-style voluntarism in which the individual or family unit chooses a "denomination" (literally, a group with a name) or a congregation to "join." So what is the relationship of "joiners" today with the "ascriptive" practices and religious culture of the past? What prevents voluntary borrowing of "bits and pieces" of traditions from becoming, as Nora suggests, a superficial manipulation, an artifice of cultural memory disconnected from the genuine experience of previous generations?

In 2009 the diocese reorganized and merged all the Catholic parishes, with all Masses and activities conducted in the newest of the Roman Catholic buildings, St. Anthony of Padua (the 1958 building for the Italian parish). Parallels with consolidated public schools come to mind, for now the whole of North Adams became a single parish, with the city itself comprising the "neighborhood" of the house of worship. The bishop declared an entirely new name for this consolidated parish, St. Elizabeth of Hungary, intended to appeal to all groups (or at least be neutral to them) with the Hungarian saint's traditional image of self-giving service. New signs were erected immediately to present to the public this new name. But can a diocese just announce the renovation of collective memory and the institution of new folkways?

Parishioners questioned the new name, partly in jest and partly in protest, strikingly on ethnic grounds. "I don't think North Adams has ever had more than two Hungarians in our whole history," one loyal and active lay member told me with a wry smile. But she goes to Mass anyway, gazing on a central platform that now holds the ornate wooden Gothic pulpit chairs from St. Francis, the elegantly etched gold candlesticks from Notre Dame, and the trim, angular 1950s Modernist marble pulpit and altar rails of St. Anthony. The furniture bears the story of broken narratives and a jumble of pieces from which the puzzle of a new narrative could be assembled.

Meanwhile, the houses of worship vacated by the ethnic "national" parishes stood silent in reproof of what might have been. In his two terms as mayor, Richard Alcombright found himself in a peculiar position as a practicing Roman Catholic who wanted to save the two major vacated houses of worship (St. Francis and Notre Dame) with their signature steeples dominating the city skyline. Alcombright is a banker by profession and has been a lay officer for parish finance successively in the parishes of Holy Family about a mile west of Monument Square on Route 2; Notre Dame; St. Francis; and now St. Elizabeth of Hungary. He has watched as each parish successively has closed, consolidating into St. Elizabeth, which now bears a new burden. While Notre Dame is actually owned by the city, St. Francis was still owned by the diocese and had to pay city property taxes since it no longer had a religious use. The longer the mayor held out for someone to buy the building and save it, the more taxes his own (consolidated) parish had to pay annually. But he persisted in the hope that this heritage could be saved, until the bitter end for St. Francis when bricks began to fall and the building was legally condemned as unsafe. The main house of worship of St. Francis was demolished in 2016 leaving a yawning gap in vistas of the city skyline along Center Street, from across the city, and even beyond from the surrounding hills. Only the parish house remains.

V.
THE PUBLIC PLACE OF HISTORIC HOUSES OF WORSHIP

"It's like losing an old friend who, over the years, hosted us as guests." [The Reverend Joe Rigali at the closing of St. George Catholic Church after 120 years, *Cincinnati* magazine August 1993]

Religious buildings, their spaces and programs, their very presence, have long been essential elements of the sense of place that grounds community life in America. The sense of place is an elusive but unmistakable quality. It is evoked in the way the natural landscape (hills and valleys, soil and streams, vegetation and climate) shape and interact with human uses (settlements and industry, farming and logging), making a life and inhabiting the land as a human community. In any town or city I visit, my first question is always, "Why is this here? Why did human beings settle in this particular place?"

And in North Adams this is certainly because of the Hoosic River and the surrounding valley, a relatively flat bowl surrounded by steep and heavily wooded hills and mountains. Here the natural elements had become a resource for human habitation that began many centuries ago with Native American civilization. Migrants of European heritage have accelerated human settlement and activity now for almost 250 years—a blip in geological time, but a relatively long stretch in the context of European settlement. In that period, North Adams has ebbed and flowed as an industrial and cultural site influenced greatly by economic forces from outside its valley.

If, as Wallace Stegner suggested, the sense of place accrues over time like a "coral reef" (themselves now endangered, one might add), houses of worship through their years of use come to embody continuity with generations who have gone before in this locale. The sense of place is embedded in the land on which they are erected; in the siting of buildings and the spaces between them and their surroundings; in vistas of steeples, towers, columns, and doorways; in the wood, slate, stone, and brick of which they are constructed. It is generated by the flows and interactions of people who have used, passed by, or come to count on the built landscape for markers of where they are in the world.

Houses of worship contribute to a sense of place well beyond the religious intentions of the congregations that build them. In intangible ways that are expressed in varied religious and civic language, they sustain collective memory and heritage. Religious groups intent on their own practices and fellowship often do not seem to understand or realize that the surrounding community also experiences their buildings, and not necessarily in terms of their doctrine and practice. Houses of worship are among the most monumental buildings in a town or neighborhood. While many non-member residents have been inside for rituals, many others know the building only as a landmark, as an element of accustomed vistas, or as a symbol of community character.

"North Adams was a *place*," reminisced a long-time journalist in his interview with Joe Manning. "It was like coming into a door on the Hadley Overpass [Route 8 from the south]. Then you were in a room that was created by the mountains, and the room had furniture which was the church steeples." Another reporter told Manning of a return visit after moving away.

> North Adams is the one place in the world that I feel comfortable in . . . I looked around, and I thought, 'Looking at this place, there's no way to decide what era I'm in. I hope we never lose this.' . . . There's a haunting quality of melancholy that still lingers here. If we let go of the past, the city will wind up being just another place. I hope they try to preserve buildings rather than destroy them.

Thus religious buildings have had a more public role than members of their congregations have often acknowledged. In many cases, certainly in the

19th century, their builders explicitly intended such a role. Construction of a house of worship using a monumental architectural style made a public argument about the role of religion in a community. As capitalist business ventures advanced through a burgeoning industrial economy, religious groups viewed their buildings as rhetorical assertions, expressed through architecture and design, that monetary gain was balanced by moral purposes. The steeples soared to a level equal to or above the factory chimneys. They announced that material or consumer values did not hold exclusive domain here, that spiritual and moral values ultimately guided the people who lived in this community. Industry was in the service of building a society of safe and healthy homes and an educated people. A North Adams observer in 1909 ascribed the prominence of their beautiful religious buildings to "the high degree of mental and moral development among the citizens." The well-being of the church and the city were inseparable. Houses of worship were essential to a thriving civic life.

At the dedication of the North Adams Congregational Church in 1865, for example, the Reverend Addison Ballard in his address took note of the mills, agricultural fairground, and nearby campus of Williams College. He stated that this "happily-completed building" for worship was that by which all other buildings were "crowned and glorified," the "keystone in the arch" of the built landscape. "Without this," Ballard said, "agriculture, manufactures, commerce, finance, art and education would make of man only a more intelligent, highly cultivated animal . . . we have come rejoicingly to this house and to all that higher good for which it stands."

When the North Adams Congregationalists celebrated their 75th anniversary in 1902, former pastor Theodore Munger highlighted "the part taken by the churches in the town in providing it with institutions" by organizing and raising funds for a library and a hospital. "Few communities have been more thoroughly dominated by the churches," he asserted. "If I were to name the chief characteristic of this church in all its history," Munger continued, "it would be—a deep interest and quick responsiveness in all matters pertaining to the welfare of the community . . . [a] sense of responsibility for the general well-being of the town."

Similarly, the primary benefactor of St. John's (now All Saints) Episcopal Church and the moving force behind the erection of its new architect-designed building in 1868 was Mrs. Elizabeth Tinker Sibley. A native of North Adams, Mrs. Sibley lived most of her life in Rochester, New York, where her husband, Hiram Sibley, was head of the newly consolidated Western Union telegraph company. Mrs. Sibley balanced her husband's commercial acquisitions with philanthropy in support of many causes around Rochester, but also to her home town parish of St. John's, "for the benefit of individuals and institutions" in a rapidly growing industrial and commercial society.

The question now is whether the public role of church buildings can be recast with imagination that connects past and future. North Adams residents, newer and longer-time, hold their houses of worship dear whether or not they participate in them in any way. One day I was standing across the street taking a photo of the fine 1929 Craftsman Gothic (now former) United Methodist Church when a middle-aged "white" man with a briefcase strode by on his way downtown. "They used to have pinnacles on that tower, you know," he announced after a brief good morning. "They had to take them down because the tower is too weak now." Who was this passerby? Not a church member, but a resident for whom these grand structures of brick and stone are landmarks to keep track of as their future becomes more uncertain.

Religious buildings are among the more significant public structures that constitute what Christopher Alexander termed the "pattern language" of a street or district. The shape of buildings, their siting close to or back from the street, their mass and height, the voids and vistas they create through their relationship with other buildings, as well as the flow of pedestrian or motorized traffic through the streets around them, are all elements in creating a distinct pattern language. The pattern becomes a taken-for-granted order of sensations as people pass regularly along; and it becomes a language as it represents and replicates the spatial and kinetic relationships of businesses, schools, theaters, government buildings, houses of worship, residences, and many other kinds of structures. The pattern language may be similar to other places—the clustering of monumental houses of worship in or near a town center, for example, or the flow of streets to a central square of a courthouse or town common—yet the pattern is also uniquely expressed in each place following the distinctly local dynamics of land and economic and social development.

So it is that the monumental buildings of 19th century North Adams became nodes of physical and visual flow as people moved through the streets. At the time most of them were built, Main Street was one of few broad boulevards in town, culminating up the hill from the Hoosic River in the open space of Monument Square (with the requisite Union soldier statue erected on a pedestal in the center). Surrounding Main Street and the Square was a tightly packed warren of streets with few structures over three to five stories in height—except for the towering steeples of religious practice. Taken together with the natural setting in a river valley within a bowl of surrounding mountains, the structures and kinetics of the built landscape gave the city its intangible character.

Preservationists around the world have debated ways to articulate "intangibility." Hungarian architect András Roman captured it as human inhabitation and presence within a natural and built environment, which over time in a particular place generates a distinct character greater than the sum of the tangible components. Food, festivals, ceremonies, handicrafts, schools, religious assemblies, and gathering places all contribute to this character. But as Portuguese architect Joao Campos argued, intangibility is really "the domain of the inexplicable" that is not easily named or verified—yet no historic streetscape is without it. Individual monuments can stand alone without human habitation, becoming artifacts of the human past; museums can create boundaries to try to accumulate and contain the artifacts of time—or all times—within a built space. But an inhabited place like a city sustains a common intangible character, a *genius loci* or spirit of place that evolves and changes constantly over time but always with an abiding continuity of past and present.

Intangibility is deeply affected by any loss. When "urban renewal" funded by Federal Government grants swept through the city in the 1960s and '70s, many of the human-scale streets of downtown North Adams were demolished, leaving some of the houses of worship standing isolated from the pattern in which they originally made sense. The pattern language of downtown was totally disrupted.

As Lou Cuyler, longtime writer for the *North Adams Transcript*, suggested to Joe Manning:

> Suppose in the urban renewal project, instead of just cutting a swath and putting up modern buildings, they had been much more selective. Suppose there had been a good master plan for the city, and that they had recognized that this room called North Adams had to be refurnished, but you didn't want to lose the ambiance

of the room. Suppose they had gotten rid of some of the old furniture, but they had spruced up the other old furniture. Instead of going toward the big anchor store, suppose they had believed in the whole concept enough to persuade banks that small was better. Instead, what they did was take that room, that wonderful room, and throw out all the old furniture and put in modern furniture. It didn't work. That's what happened in North Adams.

A pattern language is subtle, often experienced as an intangible feeling, but it is expressed in explicitly concrete ways in the actual built streetscapes and their relationship with each other.

For many inhabitants the destruction was devastating to their world of assumptions and memories. The path from home to church, once a sequence of familiar shops, cafes, hotels, and after-work hangouts, was now a blank and forbidding expanse of empty asphalt and faceless chain stores. The congregation could still be a haven of memories. Yet participants were beginning to recognize that a more metaphorical "pattern language" in which home, family, school, recreation, and church fit snugly into a flow of relationships and activities was also being disrupted by social change. The intangible ties that bound the varied social flows of the community were loosening like the streets around them.

Today's North Adams is a shape-shifting shadow of the 19th century city. The built landscape of the city eerily serves a population that is just over half what it was in 1910–13,000 people living in a built landscape intended for 25,000. Of course, the city's current population is still about a tenth of Berkshire County's 130,000, a number that has been stable for years in this mostly rural and small-town county with many second homes, resorts, and summer cultural festivals. The city's poverty rate is higher than the state or county average; the median household income much lower. The percentage of college graduates living in the city is lower than the state or county average, and the populace is somewhat older and "whiter" with less diversity of non-European ethnicities than Massachusetts as a whole.

The major industries have closed or moved to other cities or other countries since World War II. Much of the economic and social capital of North Adams evaporated with the last exodus of larger companies and jobs, most notably Sprague Electric Company, in the 1980s. As a member of First Congregational Church viewed it, the middle and upper-middle class professionals and managers—the people most likely to be active in "community service" by serving on boards of directors, church councils, and fund-raising activities—had largely moved away. The Sprague Electric collection of massive industrial buildings presented an astonishing opportunity for MASS MoCA, and key leaders of North Adams helped attract the museum to town. Yet most of the leadership and capital for rehabilitation and reuse of mill and manufacturing buildings had to come from outside the city.

Participation in the churches continues to shrink. Of the nine houses of worship within six blocks of Monument Square downtown, one has been demolished and three have been converted to other uses—one as a college auditorium and music department office, two as independent art and performance spaces. The French Roman Catholic buildings are padlocked. The Congregationalists are vigorously seeking other organizational partners to lease or share their facilities. In 2008 they sold Theodore Munger's 1888 parsonage on Church Street and now are seeking to sell their 1960s education wing. They found a buyer for their Tiffany stained glass windows and those works of art are now removed, in an effort to keep their building and remain financially viable.

The growing national trend toward abandonment and sale has raised a whole new range of questions about the public role of houses of worship. In terms set out by cultural geographer Denis Cosgrove, the landmark religious buildings could be taken to represent the once "dominant" landscape of the 19th century economic and social order. The churches to a great degree mirrored and reinforced the social stratification attendant to growing industries: the several Catholic parishes served the needs of immigrant labor from Quebec, Ireland, and Italy while Protestant churches served middle and upper management. The synagogue (originally located in a now-demolished building on Center Street) was spiritual home for Jewish merchants. While this portrayal is too simplistic and has many more nuances than this, clearly the monumentality of the houses of worship was inseparable from the industrial growth of the city, connected by rail to the global markets of an emerging large-scale factory and corporate economy. The churches in particular could represent the "official" urban ideal for an industrial city, while inadvertently or sometimes explicitly reinforcing what Cosgrove called the "excluded" landscapes of the poor, or temporary workers, or people of color.

The arrival of 75 young Chinese men from San Francisco in June 1870 hired to replace striking shoe workers provides a vivid example. Newspapers from the local North Adams *Transcript* to the New York *Tribune*, and magazines from *Scribner's* to *Harper's* to the *Independent*, puzzled over these "Celestials" and their exotic, though threatening, cultural differences. Led by their then little-known pastor Washington Gladden, some members of First Congregational Church volunteered to help the workers learn some English, and a class was organized to teach them about Christianity. But this could not counter the overall unease of the town's population stirred by everyone from workers backing a union movement to white collar citizens wanting a stable social order. This particular "excluded" landscape never fully materialized and within a decade almost all Chinese workers had left, many moving back to China and some to the budding community of Chinatown in Boston.

Today the houses of worship join the old mills and factories as markers of what Cosgrove called the "residual" landscape of an earlier society. The industries that so sharply divided management and labor and reinforced the stratification of household incomes are mostly gone. The churches are physical evidence of this older social order even as their congregations have strived valiantly to move away from old assumptions about who belongs where. The challenge is to find constructive ways for a new form of congregational life to make a home in a residual structure, parallel to the conversion of factories toward the arts and creative economy.

What is to be done in a town like North Adams? The possibility that comes immediately to mind for a city that is remaking its economy as a destination for the arts would seem to be to adapt available religious buildings for creative uses, as art schools and studios and performance spaces. This sustains their character as public gathering spaces, even if some jarring juxtapositions result. The former synagogue on Church Street, for example, was constructed in 1962; an external masonry wall facing the major thoroughfare featured a menorah of contrasting color built into the bricks—an artifact of the residual landscape—while the state college that now owns it (Massachusetts College of Liberal Arts) uses it for lectures and concerts.

New York artist Eric Rudd was one of North Adams's pioneers in rehabbing industrial and religious buildings for cultural uses, setting up a large-scale exhibit in the 1990s in the former Universalist Church building—a handsome Prairie style structure built in 1893 of Roman brick with stylish porticos and dormers. He suggested to me in an interview that actually the prospect of three or four vacant buildings was better than just one, that a whole compound of buildings adapted for use of arts and crafts could be created more easily from multiple structures. Indeed in 2013 he acquired the former United Methodist building and now has established a gallery there as a branch of the Berkshire Art Museum. Together with the former Universalist building the two sites create the possibility of just such adaptive use, standing within view of each other and just a short stroll apart across Monument Square.

Another approach to reuse would be to try to ride the crest of the "turn toward the local" that marks various forms of reaction to a globalized economy and possibly indicates signs of a new way of life. Perhaps houses of worship could become elements in what Cosgrove termed the "emergent" landscape of a place, by being absorbed into the same shift of thinking that has people trying to buy only food grown within 50 miles of home, or (re-)establishing farms and small businesses that can make a local economy thrive. A turn to the local would be somewhat ironic if one views the historic church buildings as physical expressions of a growing 19th century global economy. But such residual landscapes have often been remade and reoriented to the local in human societies.

In fact, a recent study conducted by the Berkshire Regional Planning Commission brought together varied stakeholders in Berkshire County to develop a new county-wide plan for the future. While the arts in particular are thriving in individual towns up and down Route 7 (Stockbridge, Lenox, Pittsfield, Williamstown, and adjacent towns like North Adams), the study suggested that the county still lacked a coherent message that would tie all the towns together (the self-sufficiency syndrome of New England towns persists). The published study was titled "Sustainable Berkshires" and included a section on historic preservation as a resource for sustainable communities. In particular, "new food-related industry" based on expanded local farming could make use of historic houses of worship with their commercial-grade kitchens. Some have even suggested working toward getting the county mentioned in the same breath as Napa Valley, Vermont, Cape Cod, and other regions that have branded themselves as integrating natural, social, and cultural elements toward a more locally-based sustainable way of life. The breathtaking expansion of MASS MoCA under the longtime directorship of Joseph Thompson has stirred imagination for this kind of remake of North Adams's historic downtown.

Large-scale renovation and reuse pokes at a sore spot, however, that has been festering in North Adams for years. The long-time residents who labored in the factories, managed the operating companies, or worked in service industries, and who today largely populate the declining membership of the churches, comprise the "remnant" of the formerly "dominant" social order, and the newer creative economy residents who buy the live-work lofts in the old mills and who open galleries and craft shops in vacant storefronts downtown comprise the "emergent" town. Many efforts are underway to bridge these populations; MASS MoCA puts on numerous events for the local public; new residents have been welcomed into many neighborhoods especially as they fix up the 19th century houses.

The still-active congregations meeting in the historic church buildings have not yet found a consistent way to attract new participants, with the exception of First Baptist with its multi-media style of worship. All struggle to connect with newcomers even through the arts, which would seem to be their natural partner. Without such relationships now, the passing of a beloved building from one use to another, from one collective memory to a new cultural legacy, may seem a form of alienation more than a model of partnership.

Meanwhile a new congregation has been planted in the historic 6-story Kimball Building on Main Street, under the umbrella of the Acts 29 network. The church shares its name with a few others in the region, and the choice is striking under the circumstances: Terra Nova. New earth, new land, "new ground" (as they translate it); a new generation, with new-comers including artists. And their church slogan is "Life, Place, Meaning."

The essential sense-of-place question in the religious landscape of North Adams is inescapable:

"What kind of place is this, and what place will it become?" And who gets to own or answer this question? These tensions of residual and emergent landscapes, though, express a much longer heritage of contestation that enfolds religious buildings.

VI.
HOUSES OF WORSHIP AS CONTESTED SPACES

"If only one—just one—closed church in each diocese were designated as the 'religious arts center,' perhaps there would be less acrimony over whose church was closed (and whose saved) and more of a sense of communal sharing." [Kevin T. Di Camillo, Catholic Digest, October 2017 (51)]

No material object captures the aspiration to stability and continuity of a religious tradition more than a house of worship. In a 2002 review essay of books exploring "Sacred Space in North America," historian Peter Williams challenged recent "hermeneutics of suspicion" that have predominated in some interpretations of sacred spaces and sites. David Chidester and Edward Linenthal, for example, argued that sacred space has three attributes: ritual activity, a focus on central human questions, and its "inevitably contested" character as varied stakeholders vie for the power to define (or deny) the identity and force of its sacrality. Williams replied that the interpretive frame of "contestation" was not useful for those Americans who "regard the spaces at which they attend weekly worship to be part of the ordinary patterns of their lives rather than the objects or symbols of conflicts with their neighbors." How could spaces of such ritual and regularity, continuous across time and across the shared life of fellow believers, helpfully be viewed as contested?

A closer look at historic houses of worship, though, demonstrates that the frame of contestation and sublimated or explicit conflict is a most illuminating way to interpret and understand the dynamics of these buildings. Congregations have always fussed and fumed over their buildings—how much to spend on them, how to manage and govern them, whether to expand them, to sell or to keep plugging along in the same facilities. Houses of worship are contested spaces from the time they are erected throughout their years of use. The contending forces within and around their walls normally engage in creative friction as they strive to embody their religious traditions through the wood, brick, and stone that shelter and embody their practices. When these contending forces are thrown out of balance, however, particularly when closure, sale, or demolition threatens the preservation of the building and the sense of continuity that its constituencies attach to the site, conflict over religious buildings breaks out from sublimated postures into heated and wounding struggles over identity and meaning.

Houses of worship are so numerous in North America that most people simply take for granted the freedom of religious expression in which their omnipresence makes sense. One of the unexamined assumptions undergirding the proliferation of religious buildings was simply that there was room for everyone, that land was available, that space could be found in the built landscape. By contrast with the congestion and rigid social order of their homelands, immigrants from Europe hoped and expected that they would find an open place here for religious expression. After generations of enslavement and constant displacement, African-Americans sought and expected to find a distinct place in the land (though often assuming ownership of buildings constructed by those same European-Americans now migrating elsewhere). In fact, every immigrant group from Mexico to Korea to Russia to Syria has been drawn to this land in part because there is simply room, space in which to live, to work, and to practice cultures and beliefs.

When this deeply embedded assumption of space and the honoring of freedom proves not to be true today, for example, where land is scarce or zoning regulations prevent religious or public uses in certain neighborhoods, religious groups complain that their constitutional right to "free exercise" of religion, that is, to build or expand their facilities for that "exercise," is being violated. Many resist even public efforts to preserve the unique site and place of their historic buildings through historic and landmark designations for fear of losing autonomy over their own property. Similarly Native Americans, the aboriginal migrants, have fought to protect their sacred sites, often on public land, against permits and sales that bring an influx of new settlements and industries of extraction.

Every congregation likewise has assumed equal access to the marketplace of building materials—wood, stone, brick, glass—from which to construct a building. Few congregations ever questioned this market; if a congregation could raise the money, then it would buy the needed materials. The fact that these materials were becoming scarce over a hundred years ago, that, for example, the wooden beams used for floor joists or rafters came from the last of such trees to be found in North America, did not slow congregations from competing in the building marketplace.

Religious expression itself, of course, also functioned as a marketplace. Each congregation as it built was also declaring that if "we" have a right to build here, so do others. Implicitly each congregation's physical presence recognized the presence of others. Every group that could muster the resources and get title to a piece of land and push its building plan past the city planning department and building inspectors had a common right to put up a public structure for its own form of worship. And then let the friendly competition begin, a competition that expresses itself in everything from the aggressiveness of church league softball to strategizing and marketing to attract more members.

Most debate about houses of worship within denominations or the congregations themselves focuses on this competition for members and money. The typical Protestant discussion is grounded in market assumptions about the self-sufficiency of local churches. If a congregation cannot raise enough money to maintain their historic church building, it is assumed to be their fault and their problem—obviously they do not have enough members giving money or enough "stewardship" among the members they have. And if they don't have enough members, obviously they have failed to attract new people. They are not "successful" in the local religious marketplace. If the local church property is held in trust for a denomination, then judicatory officials, conferences, or other regional bodies may act to terminate the congregation and close the building—an act usually regarded as a sign of decline and failure for the denomination in the religion market.

The typical Roman Catholic discussion begins equally from the market assumption of scarce resources. A local church building is primarily a site for Mass, which it is the responsibility of the diocese to provide. Many of these sites were created to serve a specific neighborhood, echoing the parish system of Europe. Strong remnants of this system live on, despite the constant mobility of Americans and the shifting demographics of urban areas. If there are not enough parishioners in regular attendance at Mass or to contribute to building maintenance, however, then as steward (and holder of deeds) of all the property in the diocese the bishop may decide to close that building and arrange for the remaining parishioners to join the Mass in another place. Parish councils can contest the bishop's decision based on their duties under canon law, but if they can't produce participating and contributing parishioners they are not likely to prevail.

Cries of anguish have echoed across the land over the last generation as Roman Catholic dioceses have closed parishes by the thousands. While the cries have been most acute from parishioners themselves, leading to lawsuits, pray-ins, and appeals to the Vatican, surroundings neighborhoods—the literal "parish"—have also been vociferous in protest. "The fates of parishes and wider neighborhoods are closely aligned," the *Boston Globe* editorialized in 2003.

> After closing 48 parishes over the last 18 years, the archdiocese is accustomed to emotional responses from parishioners. Now the church is also facing hardheaded public officials who link the health of parishes, especially urban parishes, with key social services and citywide efforts to improve public safety . . . the loss of a respected central institution such as a church or community center can quickly lead to disinvestment and neighborhood destabilization.

North Adams and neighboring Williamstown together have now lost five parishes, and the nearby city of Pittsfield has lost six. Four of the eleven buildings have been converted to residential housing and four others to some form of social service. Only one has been purchased by a worshiping congregation. Is the scale of these closings indicative of social change and accelerating dispersal of ethnic and neighborhood cohesion? Or do the closings themselves exacerbate these trends? Or both? The new uses may meet the deed restrictions of compatibility with the teachings of the Roman Catholic Church, but do they make a comparable contribution to neighborhood well-being if they are no longer public gathering spaces hosting diverse programs and events? Clearly a deeper understanding and constructive response requires collaboration of businesses and non-profits, local government and churches, worshippers and community constituencies.

A significant assumption undergirding the marketplace framework is the status of religious buildings as private property. To be sure, houses of worship are erected on public streets and almost all put up a permanent sign somewhere on the lot announcing their name, usually their denominational affiliation, often the schedule of services, and sometimes the pastor's name. Such signage is much less common in Europe or Britain, where national churches predominate and everyone just knows what they are. But in America, congregations announce their particular identity and practice to the public, implicitly stating that they are public gathering places where—at least theoretically—anyone may visit.

The actual names of religious properties are especially indicative of their social placement. Protestant houses of worship bearing a number—primarily

First, but also Second, Third, Fourth, and so on—are announcing not only an historical sequence of foundings, but often also their place in the community. Americans historically expected a First church to be in or near a town center and to be "civic" in nature, its members individually and collectively engaged with the civic life of the town. They were assumed to be among the most open to hosting public gatherings not limited to members of the congregation and to embrace a membership active in multiple voluntary organizations. Similarly buildings with the name of the neighborhood (Brookhaven, Lafayette Park, Queen Anne) identified themselves with the surrounding community in a pattern resonant with a parish paradigm. Houses of worship bearing the name of a founding figure of the tradition (Wesley or Luther, for example) might be assumed to be somewhat more inwardly focused on the practices derived from their own tradition, as might buildings with a biblical or theological name (Bethel, Mt. Pisgah, Trinity, Redeemer, Pentecostal) or a claim of polity and practice (Covenant, Baptist).

Despite their public signage and community presence, though, houses of worship are private property, none owned or supported by any government anywhere in the U.S. for nearly 200 years now. The internal affairs of congregations are private. Like other property owners, they can make decisions about their property without public consultation (within the bounds of local ordinances). This paradox of public space configured by private ownership is endemic to the market in American religious buildings, and one of the unspoken but persistent conflicts embedded in them.

Decisions to close church buildings and put them up for sale expose all the market assumptions about the church. Denominations and congregations appear to be saying that what they do with their buildings is solely their decision—"we own them, they serve our mission, when we're done we can sell them to any buyer we choose." Church buildings are enmeshed in what Chidester and Linenthal called (drawing on Gerardus Van der Leeuw) a "politics of property." Built as sites in which religious groups can exercise their "ownership of the 'intellectual property' of religious symbols, myths, or rituals" of their traditions, they are physical properties owned by a group that holds a deed like every other property owner. That is, in the end they are real estate. They are peculiar buildings of interest mainly to specialized buyers, but finally they are private properties with market value.

Such assumptions have limited usefulness in North Adams today, or urban neighborhoods like Holy Corners in St. Louis, or many other cities, towns, and rural crossroads across the U.S. There is no real estate market in North Adams for seven monumental houses of worship within a few blocks of each other. The United Methodist property was valued for insurance purposes at $1.1 million. But such numbers mean little to prospective buyers. The eventual contract price for the Methodists' prized house of memory was $125,000—less than many single-family houses on nearby streets. Similarly, St. John's United Methodist Church in St. Louis sold in 2014 for $930,000 or $49 per square foot, while the Residences at Holy Corners, townhomes now under construction next door, are listed at $240 per square foot.

Ironically, a building's location in an economically depressed area can be its greatest protection. As its market value sinks, the chances of its being sold or demolished sink with it. Preservation by neglect has long been recognized as a somewhat perverse tool that at least buys time for restoration or rehabilitation to get started.

By contrast, booming urban neighborhoods flourishing with new office and condominium towers, reborn city streets, and a rush of restaurants, bars, and coffee houses, present the opposite problem. Here a developer makes an offer a congregation or judicatory simply cannot refuse; the sellers can take their dollars and start something new, somewhere else. What follows are sometimes radical renovations or even demolition over which the sellers have no control.

This powerful market motivation partly explains the heated resistance of many religious groups to historic designation that might prevent their buildings' demolition or even adaptive use. There's an intriguing shadow line between the congregation that seeks National Register designation for its public stature and visibility (thus reinforcing the loyalty of members and the attraction for newcomers), and the congregation that rejects or fights designation on the assumption that their refusal will somehow enhance the market value of the property. At times this line is contested even within the same congregation as the desires of one generation conflict with the next.

As the situation of historic churches becomes more urgent across the U.S., clearly the time has come to challenge the prevalent real estate assumptions. We need to think differently, and with fresh imagination, about our built heritage. This is an element in a larger need to find new ways to calculate the values and costs of sustaining (or failing to sustain) our cultural heritage. Only then can church constituencies, preservationists, and citizens find the language to converse with each other and work together creatively to save these significant places.

Market assumptions would call for the city center churches of North Adams to consolidate or close, with their buildings put up for sale. Some would eventually be demolished and replaced with commercial or residential buildings. In fact, as church buildings across the U.S. that stand vacant today are gradually torn down, it is only consistent with the pattern of transience and disposability that has typified American society in every era. Many of the stylish neo-Gothic or Romanesque church buildings of the late 19th and early 20th centuries themselves replaced older houses of worship, many of which were routinely demolished.

What distinguishes the contemporary situation is not only the sheer number of fine structures that are at risk, but the manifest costs of not saving them. Congregations understandably talk a lot about the expense of keeping historic buildings open, and indeed, the price tag for heating, tuckpointing, putting on a new roof, and making an old building accessible can seem out of reach. The North Adams United Methodists discovered in a building audit that they faced over $1.2 million in immediate repairs. Many congregations like theirs can marshal the resources only for emergencies. All other maintenance is deferred—the costs are simply too much to manage.

But what about the costs of not saving historic houses of worship? Some of these costs are tangible. Many buildings are made of local materials. The skin of the building is often limestone, granite, coquina, or other unique stone from nearby quarries. The framing and floors are often oak, maple, walnut, or pine logged from nearby forests. These materials are for the most part irreplaceable. White pine in the North and heart pine in the South simply no longer exist—not in living trees, only in the milled wood of old buildings. In North Adams, the (former) United Methodist building alone has a wood plank ceiling and wooden rafters in the sanctuary, wood wainscoting throughout the sanctuary as well as two dining rooms and hallways, and substantial wood window frames and moldings in its classroom wing. Masters of crafts in marble, plaster, glass, wood and stone, such as found in the high-design All Saints Episcopal Church, are few and far between. Moreover, incalculable energy fueled by wood, coal, or oil went into the manufacture of materials and decorations and construction of the building. To shovel most of that into a landfill in today's world of diminished natural resources is unconscionably wasteful.

Other costs are more intangible. Denominations and congregations make public statements with their buildings, declaring with grand sanctuaries and tall steeples that they are planted in the built landscape to uplift and serve the community. Ironies abound when they now declare that their buildings are just private property and that they have the same prerogative as any property owner to dispose of a building without public consultation. A Roman Catholic bishop or a United Methodist annual (regional) conference, a congregation or even a pastor alone, can close a church at a rural crossroads or an urban intersection without consulting other parishes, conferences, neighborhood groups that meet in the building, or public officials working toward revitalization of the community in which the building is located. But a decision to close, sell, or demolish a church building can come at devastating cost to the larger community.

Thus a little-discussed but persistent way in which houses of worship are contested spaces is embodied in their community context, the built landscape and the people that inhabit it. Greater exploration and constructive resolution of the conflict between religious groups and local communities will require a much richer and more critical perspective on houses of worship within the built environment. From this perspective may issue increasingly creative solutions for the preservation and use of these buildings for the whole community.

Clues to a new way of thinking are embedded, ironically, in the North Adams town "brand." The church buildings belong to the whole community; they are an asset to the whole "City of Steeples." Their future must be managed, not foremost around assumptions of private property on the real estate market, but around their significance to the social and cultural life of the city. Approaches to saving these buildings for continued use will be found in exploring the many ways they contribute—through their spaces, their activities, their beauty—to the social good of the community. One concrete way to gain recognition of these contributions is to monetize them; Partners for Sacred Places conducts studies of the "Halo Effect" of congregations, for example. Done thoroughly, these studies will demonstrate how critical religious buildings are for the local economy.

A persistent question of vision and imagination troubles any such solutions, though. The blunt and plain-speaking former mayor of North Adams, John Barrett, decried in his interview with me what he considered the lack of "leadership" among religious groups. "I have to put together a strategy for them," the mayor declared. "I wrote a letter [about Notre Dame] to the diocese—it took over a year to get a response." Then, much to his professed surprise, representatives of other denominations began to come to the mayor's office. "I never thought the Protestants would be here to see me," he said. "I thought they had large endowments."

Church buildings are "the history of this community." He demurred, "It's not a religious point of view . . . it's aesthetics . . . [losing the buildings would] change the character of downtown . . . [it's a matter of] saving our history." So when he was mayor he was working with a local bank to create a temporary fund so that the city could buy and hold vacated houses of worship until a buyer could be found to rehabilitate them for new uses. Ultimately, though, the city could afford to acquire only the Notre Dame property and has had to hold it for lack of a buyer for over a decade.

Several years before it closed, St. Francis parish sold the building across the intersection that had housed the order of nuns who taught in the parochial school, St. Joseph's, itself now closed and converted to senior housing. The convent was purchased by the Brooks Pharmacy chain, which demolished the building to construct a new drugstore. Brooks subsequently sold to the Rite-Aid chain, which naturally drew the interest of CVS Pharmacy in buying the St. Francis church building after it was vacated. By demolishing it they could construct one of their mass-design stores on the height of land of downtown (at a considerably higher elevation than the Rite-Aid, now of course absorbed into Walgreen's).

In Mayor Barrett's opinion, the diocese sold the convent too cheap to the pharmacy corporation. But "nobody listens to the church" these days, in his view. The churches are "not respected right now" because a national corporation, for example, sees nobody in church leadership who will deal forcefully at a negotiating table. Many citizens of North Adams organized to fight demolition of St. Francis—arguably the most prominent of the steeples rising over the main intersection of Route 2 at the city center. But the diocese remained silent and invested no further money in basic maintenance. After St. Francis was demolished and the lot cleared, a CVS-type development seemed inevitable. Public awareness and resistance so far has protected the site from yet one more ugly standard-design commercial building. But can a city with so few resources resist corporate real estate overtures, or persuade the diocese to resist them?

As the chair of the local historical commission, Justyna Carlson, told me,

> We have made stands as far as 'this is Steeple City' . . . we want facilities used, not demolished. We don't have an awful lot of clout. If a congregation comes to us, we will certainly support them in trying to find a use for it. We can't do an awful lot, we just keep trying. We write letters to the editor, we go to meetings . . . Massachusetts Historic Commission lists the budget for local commissions—we get nothing while others in state are $50,000 or more.

The commission's mandate lacks any legal teeth; the city has no historic districts under local government and thus no design guidelines to prevent radical changes in historic structures. They have been able to achieve city government adoption of a one-year demolition delay after notice of intent. This helps, but not enough.

Both the city and the churches lack sufficient economic and social power to drive constructive planning. As Joe Manning remarked to me about North Adams, "People are so used to things failing." For every step forward—the growing MASS MoCA, renovation of the Holiday Inn downtown, a new restaurant here and there—something else is closed and gone. 2014 was an acutely painful year for the city. The local newspaper, the *North Adams Transcript*, merged into the regional *Berkshire Eagle* after 170 years of publication. The North Adams Hospital closed with only 24 hours' notice, a shock to the city and its employment base. The local Nassif Pharmacy shut its doors after many years at a highly visible location on Church Street.

Meanwhile, news stories and rumors are constantly circulating about plans for a new condominium development in the old Notre Dame buildings, or a new hotel on the empty asphalt of the "urban renewal mall" on Main Street, or a new museum in the old railroad buildings and yards now called Heritage Park, or a new gourmet restaurant in the vacant Church of the Incarnation (Roman Catholic) in the Blackinton neighborhood. Thomas Krens has returned to the Berkshires where he once taught at Williams College, after a world-renowned career expanding the Guggenheim Museum to multiple locations. He shared the original vision for MASS MoCA when he was at Williams, and now is said to be envisioning ways to recreate the 19th century urban landscape as a major cultural center with multiple museums and additional hotels.

Some plans come to fruition; the mid-20th century Redwood Motel near the town line of Williamstown has been converted into a high-end inn called Tourists. A new brewery has started up at the gates of MASS MoCA. A new boutique hotel seems to be underway on Eagle Street. But many times the envisioned development plans just disappear from public view; it is private property and investment after all. Local residents have long since grown an "I'll believe it when I see it" attitude.

What could make it possible for religious buildings to become part of the "emerging" landscape of a place? Can their physical presence and their resonance with collective memory be an asset in creating a functional and creative built environment for the next generation? Or will they function only as a diminished artifact, an imitative self-parody as a site of memory, in Nora's terms? These questions challenge religious groups to reconsider their decisions to walk away from their historic buildings—decisions made in the framework of the marketplace of private property—without equal consideration of the impact on the built landscape and sense of place of the community; and they challenge everyone to reimagine these buildings as a public asset. As a member of St. Francis parish put it to me, "It's terrible to just throw away our history—that's what we do in America, tear it down and build something new." The way we handle our growing stock of underutilized and vacant historic religious buildings in America will say a lot about the kinds of communities we want to have, and a great deal about the practices of the traditions that put up the buildings.

VII.
INTERPRETING RELIGIOUS ARCHITECTURE AND DESIGN

"Own a Piece of History. Originally built as a Methodist Church in 1849, this historic building is permitted for both commercial and residential use . . . It has a massive chestnut post and beam frame, situated on its original stone foundation." [http://www.hartsvilledesign.com/building-for-sale.html accessed 07/31/19]

"BACK ON MARKET—PRICE REDUCED Redevelopment Opportunity—Unique Historic Structure—41,018 square foot building on 1.55 acres of land" [Real estate packet for former St. John's United Methodist Church, St. Louis, Missouri, 2009]

The massive numbers of empty or underutilized houses of worship across the United States and other nations provoke the question of whether new uses for them can be found that resonate with contemporary society and culture, and thus continue to form the collective memory of a community—constituting a living history, not merely an archival or nostalgic one. The architecture itself is both an opportunity and a challenge for a continuing community role of religious buildings. The opportunity lies in sensations of awe and beauty provoked by these distinctive spaces—a shared sense of significance however vaguely defined. The challenge lies in shifting how we perceive the space, from a static to a dynamic sensibility that allows the building to evolve in function and meaning.

The architecture of houses of worship unquestionably can "evoke the sublime" by creating an environment that shapes the experience of observers. "It is their eventfulness in our consciousness that makes them unforgettable, profound, ineffable." Julio Bermudez and other scholars active in the symposia of the Architecture, Culture, and Spirituality Forum have conducted research on "extraordinary architectural experiences" that fundamentally alter perception, many of which occur in houses of worship. Even those who have read previously about a particular building report a "surprising and spontaneous experience" when in the presence—what Walter Benjamin termed the "aura"—of the original work of architecture and its aesthetic features. Many observers would readily call any space that evokes these sensations "sacred."

The phenomenological approach taken by Bermudez and others, supported by growing interest in linking architectural experience with neuroscientific research, does not attempt to address the long-disputed subject of what actually constitutes "the sacred." As David Chidester and Edward Linenthal summarize in their introduction to *American Sacred Space*, some scholars of religion have held an essentialist view that the sacred is ontological, that is, that the sacred has Being, that it is the Holy which human beings aspire to apprehend. Other scholars have thought such an assertion too much influenced by the monotheistic religions of the Western world. Many have articulated a more functional understanding of the sacred, that its form and place in people's lives is constructed "through the human labor of consecration" that fills the "empty signifier" of "sacred" with a language for transcendence. "This clash between substantial and situational approaches to definition and analysis represents a contrast between what might be called the poetics and the politics of sacred space," Chidester and Linenthal conclude. In the first view a place is sacred because the Holy comes to meet one there and the ineffable presence can only be articulated through inherited images and metaphors. In the second, participants construct sacred places through rituals that often lead to the politics of official spaces and approved norms.

I would propose a third view in an effort to move beyond the polarity of essentialism and social constructivism. In this more pragmatist view, places become sacred through the practices of participants over time. Practices are rooted in heritage and continue historical precedents but are also infinitely adaptable to current circumstances. Practices are performative, that is, they become what they are through the performance of them, and performances always occur at a moment in time. A pastor can perform a hundred baptisms using ritual language and each one will be different. Multiple lectors will read the same verses over time and each voice will have its unique tone and cadence. A congregation can sing the same hymn a hundred times (and some do!) and each performance at a distinct moment in time will be unique. Thus apprehension of the sacred will always be in process and will strike individual participants in different ways at different moments in their lives.

A pragmatic view mediates between extremes in which the sacred may be understood as true doctrine and belief about the Holy—an essentially ideological position—or on the other hand as plainly a construction of human beings seeking something transcendent. Pragmatism holds by contrast that while human beings embody what Pierre Bourdieu called a "*habitus*" of practices—embedded social patterns of thought and action that give order to their lives—they are also constantly adapting and innovating in the context of changing circumstances—what Bourdieu called "regulated improvisation." Practices of seeking the sacred are neither wholly locked in by tradition, official doctrine, and "correct" ways of performing rituals (enforced by approved ritual administrators) nor are practices made up from scratch at the whim of individual desire.

Pragmatism is not focused on whether claims of sacred space are "true" but rather on how participants come to see a particular space as significant in their apprehension of sacrality. Houses of worship provide a means of organizing space and time, offering a place in which to gather and times at which collective (or individual) activities will occur. They give order to the human search for substance and depth in life, and rhythm to the flow of days. True, they have been constructed in physical form that reflects the practices of the participants who built them. They create a visual field and patterns of moving through their spaces that echo the *habitus* of inherited ways. Yet they are always adaptable to new understandings, new forms, new circumstances. In this sense "sacred" is not a noun, not even an adjective, but a verb.

Greenwood Social Hall in Kansas City, Missouri, provides an intriguing example of the questions in play here. Artist and designer Peregrine Honig first saw the former Greenwood Baptist Church in 2016 after the congregation had sold it for conversion to a private residence two years earlier. Honig caught the renovation in process and decided to buy this building for her home, studio, and performance space. Basic design features of the 1927 structure were restored and the raked floor leveled, with the Social Hall name to express both the continuity of the building as a public space and its reuse for exhibits and performances.

Even after the African-American Baptist community that had built the church had moved out, their pastor, Mike Carroll, chose not to deconsecrate the building. In the words of the interviewing journalist, he "wanted the spirit that had accumulated to remain long after the congregation had left." Indeed Honig told the paper, "I really curate the space with a Baptist preacher in mind" thinking of performances as a kind of testimony. The church, she said, "has a really amazing feel . . . but also there are certain things I haven't done here because I just don't think the spirit would like it." Her practices in this case appear to be reshaping a sense of the sacred from materials both old and new.

Underwriting this pragmatist view is the insistence of Lindsay Jones in his *Hermeneutics of Sacred Architecture* that the "meanings" of religious buildings intended by their original architects and builders cannot be said to "remain fixed throughout the careers of their creations," that such works of art have "fluidity and dynamism" that cannot be contained as an "inherent, stable meaning." Whatever sensations the design was meant to provoke through the dimensionality and light of a space, or however the layout was meant to guide the eye and the feet in the pathways of ritual, the actual participants may well not experience or understand the designer's plans.

For buildings a century old or older, five or more generations of participants have come and gone; and while a certain timelessness may pervade the pattern and flow of the design, participants may gravitate toward using the rooms in ways the designer never imagined. The spaces may resonate with the practices of the past, the founding generation especially, but contemporary practitioners of the spaces cannot "'get back into' the consciousness of their creators or users." Rather, the design, the spaces, the structure, may be seen as "perpetually new."

Religious buildings should be understood, Jones argues, not as fixed in meaning but rather as "transforming, life-altering environments" that are received by successive generations in ways appropriate to new contexts and situations. Their meaning is a "negotiation . . . that subsumes both building and beholder—in the *ritual-architectural event*" of encounter. Buildings are not "inert, static objects of reflection" but rather themselves in play as "dynamic partners in conversation" for participants who engage them. This hermeneutic of buildings opens up the possibilities of houses of worship becoming ever-renewed in their experience and use.

Jones suggests that religious buildings are apprehended through multiple "protocols" or frameworks of interpretation depending on the interests of the observers or participants in a particular circumstance. The indigenous "audience" using the building for its original purpose such as worship and ritual may find the space so natural as not to require any self-conscious thought or attention. The resonance and flow of the room are a familiar and taken-for-granted environment of devotion. Meantime, an architectural historian describing the building and its design history will be attending to distinctive features that give the building its style and character and that, if removed, would diminish its integrity. And a visitor or tourist observing the building will be scanning for elements that make the space familiar, bringing to mind experiences from other places. This outsider "audience" much more than the indigenous participants will be struck by features that seem strange or difficult to understand.

Adding to the multiple protocols is a trait distinctive to most houses of worship: they are among the more complex and variegated structures in American culture. Particularly buildings constructed after the 1880s in urban neighborhoods or town centers were planned for multiple functions with spaces designed accordingly. While the worship room remained the central focus, other spaces were created to provide a variety of other services such as classrooms for education, recreational facilities (gymnasiums, swimming pools, bowling alleys), kitchens equipped to serve hundreds of meals at a sitting, large open halls for meetings and meals, formal parlors and sitting rooms for socializing, a raised stage or even theater for performances, a second more informal auditorium, and an office suite for the administration required to manage complex operations. In the 19th century such buildings were termed "institutional churches" to try to convey the comprehensive services they offered for every aspect of life—a term that morphed by the end of the 20th century into "full service churches" open for activities virtually all the time.

The diversity of spaces and uses within religious buildings is firmly rooted in ancient languages that underlie contemporary (American) English terminology. The Hebrew word for places of worship is *bayit-el* transliterated into English as *bet-el* or Bethel. *Bayit* means "house" and *bayit-el* "house of the Lord," yet *bayit* in itself must be understood as an expansive term. It embraces not only a literal place or building but a "household" inclusive of anyone who lives in the house and everyone in the family line (such as the House of Samuel or the House of David). The sense of the word reaches even farther in the term *Bet Yisrael* embracing everyone of Jewish faith.

Likewise in ancient Greek, the adopted language of Christianity, a term for church was *Kyriakos*—*Kyrios/Oikos* or house of the Lord (likely the origin of the German *Kirche* and English "church"). *Oikos* also is an expansive term of "household" going well beyond a specific place or building to include all people associated with it (such as the household of Prisca and Aquila mentioned in the Greek Testament [Romans 16:5]). The order of the household, its arrangements for sustenance and labor, was in Greek *oikonomia* (*oikos*/household—*nomos*/order) transliterated into English as economy. Over time *oikos* and the terms built upon it expanded metaphorically to name the household order or economy of a larger society or global civilization, or ecology (*oikos*/household—*logos*/language about or study of) as the exploration and study of the whole earth as a systemic household.

The dynamism of these terms as they move back and forth from the literal to the metaphorical and the local to the global is equally captured in other language about religious buildings. Synagogue is transliterated from the Greek *syn*/together—*gogein*/gathering, reflecting the dispersal of Jews through the Hellenic world and the need to have places of gathering. As Western Christianity gravitated toward Rome, the Latin term *con-gregatio* became widely used, coming into English as congregation. Here again the sense of the word is the act and practice of coming together or gathering in a place around a common purpose.

Synagogues and congregations vary across a spectrum of understandings of "household"—from strict limits of belonging, to liberality and openness of inclusion, and everything in between. Yet the expansive sense endemic to the terminology clustered around "houses of worship" evokes an interactive relationship with constituencies beyond the "membership." The language readily bursts its limits to go beyond focused concerns for order in belief and practice, to care for the economy or good order and well-being of the wider community. Clearly many houses of worship, particularly those built to accommodate a variety of services, played a central role in the cohesiveness of surrounding communities by bringing people together for a wide range of purposes and kinds of communication and encounter. Their spaces could be understood and interpreted in varied ways depending on the interests of constituencies and the activities different audiences experienced there. When compared with the singularity and uniformity of an office building, a theater, or a restaurant, they appeared to be essentially many buildings in one. Their multiplicity of uses may become even more striking in its absence, as when such a building is converted to a single use such as condominiums or offices. This kind of reductive conversion vastly diminishes the richness of the overlapping layers of meaning and practice of the building's historic purposes.

With multiple audiences and criss-crossing interpretive protocols at play, houses of worship clearly cannot be imagined as static but as living entities engaged in continuous conversations about their significance and meaning. Such buildings are both familiar and strange, both alluring and concealed, both inviting and transformative. A back-and-forth pattern, like breathing in and breathing out, marks a creative process from which a new sense of their place can emerge. As cultural geographer Anne Buttimer wrote, a sense of place builds up through a constant reciprocal movement of "home and horizons of reach . . . rest and movement, territory and range, security and adventure, housekeeping and husbandry, community building and social organization." As sites of gathering and dispersing, of social space, of the interplay of inheritance and present activity, houses of worship invite interaction, collaboration, and reciprocity.

The former St. John's United Methodist Church property in St. Louis provides a rich and complex study of architectural conversation and negotiation of meanings. Closed in 2007, the building had stood for 100 years as an exemplar of the multi-faceted "institutional church." But now the theater had to be cleared and old sets broken down; classrooms and closets cleaned out and mountains of trash hauled away; congregational records in overflowing office file cabinets and credenzas boxed and sent to the denominational archives; and most furnishings not affixed to floors or walls given or sold to other congregations. The property then was almost continuously on the real estate market until 2014.

In United Methodist polity, when congregations are discontinued their buildings revert to the annual (regional) conference of the denomination. Efforts began immediately after closing to try to create a new United Methodist congregation at the site; when that fell through, the conference trustees authorized listing the building on the real estate market for $1.3 million. But with the economic downturn of those years, no market existed for this kind of building. Congregations came to look, but flinched at the costs of maintenance and utilities. None had a constituency large enough to make use of over 40,000 square feet of worship and activity space. The price was soon reduced well below $1 million, less than the asking price of most of the 19th century mansions only a block or two away.

The task of marketing this historic house of worship fell largely to the commercial realtors of Hilliker Corporation. A building designed for worship, education, and fellowship in the traditions and practices of a particular religious heritage now had to be reinterpreted by real estate agents. Their task was to stir potential buyers to reimagine the spaces for adaptive use. One inspiration right across Washington Place was the conversion of the Temple Israel school building into state-of-the-art architects' offices, retaining the handsome stone floors and even the striking Star of David embedded in the floor of the foyer. But Second Baptist just across Kingshighway Boulevard was for sale as well, along with several other sizeable church buildings in the city. The market was already flooded.

A variety of parties besides congregations showed interest in adapting the property even though its most significant interior spaces (sanctuary and chapel) could not be altered or subdivided under the building's local historic landmark designation in the Central West End Historic District. One prospective buyer wanted to convert it to a popular music venue, complete with liquor license. The neighborhood was adamantly opposed. An established St. Louis catering business proposed using the kitchen for catering while converting the former sanctuary into an event space (thus ironically changing its purpose from wedding ceremonies to wedding receptions). When they walked away because of financial risk, a building design firm and a software company looked at it, but had no realistic proposal for the sanctuary space. Meanwhile, all the copper gutters and downspouts were stolen, allowing rainwater to accumulate in and around the basement and create a mold problem that proved to be another major expense to abate.

The diversity of potential buyers made effective reinterpretation essential. But in the longer view this would not have been the first time the building was reinterpreted. Richard Kieckhefer provided a vocabulary for interpretation of religious space in his *Theology in Stone*. He identified four basic approaches to understanding a worship space: its dynamics or sense of flow; its focal point that draws the senses; its aesthetic impact; and its symbolic resonance. A Gothic cathedral design, for example, creates a flow of energy down a nave much longer than it is wide; draws the eye to a focal point of the altar; displays designs, murals, paintings, stone carvings, stained glass, and other aesthetic features that together enhance the experience of sacrality; and collectively the preceding elements create a resonance that for adherents and non-adherents alike generally evokes the symbolic power of reverence.

In the case of Link's design for St. John's, the room was arranged as an auditorium with a sweeping curve of pews facing a broad platform with center pulpit. After World War II, just before urban congregations and institutions began to realize the devastating impact of suburbanization, the St. John's congregation remodeled, taking out the heavy wooden platform, furniture, organ case, and wainscoting that had been the focal point, and replacing it with a divided chancel, marble floor, raised pulpit, lectern, and stained glass depiction of St. John made by a local artist. While the flow continued to be a sweep across the crowd and toward the central platform, the focal point shifted to the altar—expressing liturgical reforms of the day. The symbolic resonance remained grand in scale, through the barrel-vaulted arch of the ceiling, formal classical elements such as columns and pediments along the sides, and the rich wood tones of the pews and platform furnishings. The room could still evoke awe.

Lindsay Jones's argument, that religious buildings are not "inert, static objects of reflection" but instead are partners in a conversation with those who experience and use them, now comes into play. Certainly a room like the St. John's auditorium could, over time and generations, evoke varied meanings and uses from participants. This is most explicit in the congregation's act of remodeling the worship space to suit new ritual practices. But the variation of meanings is also apparent in such subtle relations as the fact that by the 1960s, few participants remained who would have grasped the original synergies of Union Station and St. John's. The former once bustled with 100,000 passengers a day on trains pulling into one of the 32 tracks sheltered by an 11-acre single-span train shed, a mighty symbol of the economic engine of St. Louis and the Midwest. The latter was bursting from its main auditorium with the aspirations, the songs and prayers, of hundreds of business and civic leaders. The 1960s brought rapid decline in the uses of both buildings. Thus there is the hard fact that by 2007, no one remained who knew any of the donors memorialized in plaques or stenciled on the seating chart. The collective memory of the current congregation now absorbed earlier stories of the social grandeur of St. John's as a bemusing artifact of the past, and was generating its own memories as a people who were struggling to survive on a tough urban corner.

With all collective memory dispersed and gone after 2007, interpretation of the space now fell to realtors trying to market a building stripped of many elements symbolizing its original purpose. The denomination removed the platform furnishings and the St. John window above the altar. But because of the building's landmark status, windows depicting the figures of Methodist patriarchs John and Charles Wesley had to remain on either side of the main Washington Place door and the writers of the Christian gospels still towered over the pews from the south nave windows on the Kingshighway Boulevard side. Does such a room still have symbolic resonance? If so, to whom? What does an observer have to know in order to pick up the resonance? Should a realtor just ignore all this, and by redescribing the space, erase its sacrality?

The eventual buyers were the appropriately named Link Auction Galleries, Inc., dealers in high-end art and antiques. When I was last able to see the building in 2016 or hear a first-hand account in 2017, Link had converted large classroom and gathering spaces into display areas; the chapel now hosted the auctions. The many beautiful designs and artistic expressions on view did indeed have a transcendent element to them as manifestations of human aspirations and apprehensions of beauty. And perhaps this is what customers were experiencing as they walked the spaces and attended to the objects displayed in the gracious old rooms. But strikingly, Link had not found a use for the largest gathering space, the auditorium with its sweep of pews and elevated platform, its tall windows and soaring barrel vault ceiling. A large hole had developed in the plaster of the ceiling coffers, and the room appeared to be mainly a storage and staging area.

Many houses of worship around the US have been turned to other uses such as offices, restaurants, performance venues, or residences. This is a laudable means of preserving distinctive architecture and invaluable building materials as well as the visual continuity and integrity of the built landscape. At the same time, new audiences drawn by the new uses will only be one among many who apprehend the building in varied ways. I have never thought I could work or sleep in a room that retains the stained glass window of a religious tradition. But I have always been an active religious practitioner so my judgment may be skewed that direction. I just have trouble believing that the "ritual-architectural event" of engagement between religious practitioner and built environment ever entirely goes away. Then again, perhaps it simply morphs into a new ritual and thus a new spatial flow and dynamic—an orchestra performing on what had been the worship platform, for example, or a brewpub using interior columns and side aisles to create more intimate bar and dining spaces.

Grace Restaurant in Portland, Maine, offers an especially complex and poignant example for me. Located in the former Chestnut Street Methodist church in downtown Portland, the restaurant (now an event space) took as its design brand the ancient triquetra form represented in the historic windows and woodwork of the church. While the three interlocking arcs can symbolize the unity of any three elements, in Christian tradition they represent the unity of the Trinity. The restaurant also retained stained glass windows depicting scenes from the Bible, repurposed the pulpit as a host stand, and of course, adopted the name "grace," which while used widely to speak of gifts or presences that come from beyond ourselves has a decidedly spiritual overtone. So what do I think and imagine as I sit at the bar located in the center of the former nave, under an ingenious and elegant canopy floating overhead in a triquetra design that defines the bar space with the three arcs creating distinct service areas for the bartenders—and Jesus looking over my shoulder from afar as I sip my martini? For me this is a somewhat jarring experience, especially because I am a lifelong Methodist for whom the waning of dynamic downtown churches across the country has been a sharp reshaping of my reality. From another perspective, though, the complex conversation in which I am engaged with the renovated building is really no more complicated than I am as a person who is Methodist, and also a historic preservationist, and also an avid student of architecture and design, who also likes martinis.

Perhaps it is the particular gift of a building as monumental, symbolic, varied and multi-dimensional as a house of worship to generate a plenitude of means of engagement, which produces a many-faceted ritual-architectural conversation, all of which suggests that multiple adaptive uses of these historic spaces could be possible. To the range of such possible uses we now turn.

VIII.
SCENARIOS FOR HISTORIC HOUSES OF WORSHIP

"Seeking $30 million to renovate, church finds help in neighbors" [New York Times headline for news story about St. Bartholomew's Episcopal Church, Park Avenue, 2007]

"THE LINE D.C. [is] housed in a historic, neoclassical church . . . Among the most standout design features are the provocative spiky chandelier in the front lobby, which was fashioned from church organ pipes, and the pews, which have been dramatically punched up with midnight blue velvet" ["Why THE LINE DC is Washington, D.C.'s Hippest Hotel" Forbes (02/27/18) accessed 07/31/19 https://www.forbes.com/sites/katiechang/2018/02/27/why-the-line-dc-is-the-nations-capitals-hippest-hotel/#173064617758]

With the ballooning numbers of underutilized or vacant houses of worship in the US, communities across the nation face the challenge of what to do next. The time-honored

American solution, evident in the stories of churches and synagogues in growing cities or changing countrysides, is simply to tear down a structure that is no longer viable or in use. No one will ever know how many religious buildings have been demolished across the generations, a fraction of their materials and artifacts saved and reused, most of the remnants dumped in the local landfill.

But in the early 21st century, this expediency and waste is plainly no longer acceptable. As earth's resources continue on a path of drastic exhaustion, the loss of irreplaceable wood, stone, glass, plaster, and myriad other materials native to a locale is simply unconscionable. Houses of worship, however today's society views the motivations behind their construction, represent an enormous investment of energy. They tell a story of human settlement and aspiration embodied in brick and stone. Their towers and steeples, arches and steps, stand for continuity with generations that have gone before us. They are material symbols of community identity and character accrued over time.

1. Changing the Paradigm

The rationale for sustaining them in our era has shifted dramatically in recent years. Only a generation ago, the primary challenge of historic houses of worship was framed in terms of preservation. This approach, codified in municipal ordinances across the land, introduced the police powers of the state as a force to prevent demolition or significant alteration to the iconic religious buildings (and many other kinds of contributing structures, of course) in a historic or landmark district. Buildings were not to be expanded, remodeled, or altered in any way that changed their character-defining features.

Use of police powers, needless to say, led to highly publicized legal conflicts between churches and preservation agencies that captured public discourse in the 1980s and early '90s. St. Bartholomew's Episcopal Church on Park Avenue tangled with the Landmarks Preservation Commission of the City of New York over the church's proposal to erect a high-rise office building on the site of their 1928 "community house" activities building, adjacent to architect Bertram Goodhue's magnificent confection of Byzantine design and decoration in the 1918 sanctuary building. A few years later the Roman Catholic archbishop of San Antonio disputed the jurisdiction of the historic landmark commission of Boerne, Texas, over proposed expansion of the Spanish Mission-style St. Peter Church. Both cases landed in appeals courts and the latter in the Supreme Court. While preservationists "won" the legal right to designate churches as landmarks and subject them to preservation ordinances, such situations mainly demonstrated the failure of constructive conversations between churches and preservationists. Thomas F. Pike, board chair at the founding of Partners for Sacred Places and a prominent New York clergyman with a passion for preservation, even termed the climate a "war" and appealed for both sides to understand each other and work together.

The skirmishes of the 1980s still echoed well into the new century. Many religious leaders viewed historic preservation activities or any other zoning restrictions with skepticism, even disdain, declaring that legal measures unjustifiably block needed change and thus hinder the "free exercise" of a dynamic religious faith. Many religious organizations were thrilled with Congress's adoption of the omnibus Religious Land Use and Institutionalized Persons Act (RLUIPA) of 2000, which shifted the legal burden to local governments to demonstrate a clear and compelling public interest in restricting the construction or renovation activities of congregations. Thus the contest of interests was renewed.

By 2010 new court cases were springing up especially around the mass closings of Catholic parish churches. The Diocese of Springfield that includes North Adams sued to prevent the Springfield City Council from landmarking significant church buildings including Our Lady of Hope with the tallest bell tower in the city. The suit failed in both District Court and the U.S. First Circuit Court of Appeals (2013) on the grounds that the ordinance did not interfere with religious practices or impose a burden on the diocese. Subsequently the local historical commission granted permission for the diocese to remove the stained glass windows for display elsewhere as long as the window openings were not boarded up. The Cleveland (OH) Landmarks Commission likewise has strategized to prevent demolition of Catholic churches as well as alterations to their interior features such as stained glass windows; and in the case of the Church of the Transfiguration (Episcopal) finally agreed to demolition in exchange for the diocese saving the façade and narthex for design elements of some future building.

So is it more important to protect the historic character of urban districts, or more critical to protect the right of religious groups to control their own property as they see fit? Or is there a better question that does not reinforce opposing positions of religious faith on one side and preservation ethic on the other? After all, one would think the two sides had much in common—sustaining traditions, for example, or seeking beauty and elevation of the human spirit.

Today the conversation has greater possibility of becoming more collaborative and constructive. The historic preservation movement has shifted dramatically away from its original dominant ethos of protecting houses, public buildings, churches, and monuments designed by significant architects and laden with elegant craftsmanship, which inevitably were the product of rich and powerful interests. The movement now is increasingly more focused on the vitality of local communities, growing partnerships among business and community organizations to revitalize the vernacular buildings and streetscapes of a town or neighborhood. Historic structures are understood as part of landscapes that embrace land, natural features, climate, and resources necessary to sustain all forms of life. The movement is turning, in other words, much more toward an ethos of conservation. The question is not how to preserve in the sense of preventing change and freezing a building in time, but how to conserve in the sense of the continuing use of our natural and built landscapes to create a sustainable way of life.

A conservation ethic opens the way to viewing an historic house of worship within its whole setting, that is, not as an isolated chunk of private property or as an ornamental sculpture to be appreciated solely for itself (and many photos are framed or altered so as to screen out the surroundings as an intrusion on the pure form). Structures of varied height, depth, mass, and scale organically form the fabric of a streetscape, a complex and integrative whole. The fabric is woven not only by the buildings themselves but by the movements and interactions of people who move through the landscape. I like to think of each person crossing through the larger setting as trailing a ball of yarn behind them. As the various yarns cross and tangle and dip and turn, the warp and woof of the fabric takes shape. Each person, and each building through which people move, becomes a strand or knot in a web of relationships and interactions and flows that create a community in constant movement and formation. The historic house of worship in this sense holds a place as a dynamic and sometimes transformative node into which some members of a community flow for varied activities within those spaces and then, shaped by those experiences, flow back out into the community to interact in ever-changing ways. This more systemic understanding of daily life opens the way to consider how congregations can build community partnerships to help sustain the physical structure, or alternatively, how communities can absorb a house of worship into new patterns of activity that contribute to community vitality.

The impending crisis of these buildings thus presents an unmatched opportunity. Historic houses of worship, holding their place in the land for generations, can be one of the most visible forms of witness to the values and character of a community that make it healthy, vital, and just. Now, through partnerships of congregations and community institutions and organizations, the presence of these buildings can be enhanced in new patterns and uses.

In North Adams, for example, the fate of vacant houses of worship has been the catalyst for new public awareness of preservation and conservation values. The threat of losing all or part of the St. Francis property to the CVS national pharmacy chain forced the city to recognize, as noted previously, that it had no ordinance on the books empowering the city to enforce a delay in demolition of a significant building. The demolition ordinance, modeled on that of over 130 other Massachusetts municipalities, was adopted in 2013.

That action led naturally to a further realization that the city had no ordinance empowering the creation of a local historic district. North Adams has over 100 buildings and six historic districts on the National Register of Historic Places, including Monument

Square and Church Street. But the National Register places no restrictions on property owners, other than the threat of being removed from the list. Over the years since 1978, the city's Historical Commission has developed a survey of over 1000 historic properties, and continues to add properties to the survey thanks to grants from the Massachusetts Historical Commission. Yet the local Historical Commission has been advisory only and not integral to the city planning and permitting process. Today, moved by the need to protect the historic mills and churches that give the city its character, the city council may begin to consider creating a local historic district that would include police powers. An ordinance would authorize a local historic district commission mandated to review the renovation, reuse, or partial or complete demolition of any designated building in the district. Over 200 such districts exist in Massachusetts, but only two in Berkshire County in which North Adams is located.

The dearth of local historic districts, and the city's failure to empower even one over the years, reflects the fiercely independent character of the region. Property rights are deemed to be at the epicenter of living in a free society, and government restrictions on property an infringement of liberty. Yet many people now see that without a public role in guiding the future of the built landscape, the city could lose its distinctive features. An alternative could be the adoption of a historic conservation district, which though lacking in regulatory power, allows a neighborhood to define for itself what its distinctive features and character are, encourages property owners to organize to preserve those features, and brings the planning resources of the city to bear by incentivizing owners toward actions that ensure continuity of a neighborhood's distinctive character. In short, the latter is more of a "carrot" than a "stick."

Congregations and communities have a number of options to keep houses of worship viable and useful. All options suggest that historic houses of worship will find key partners in neighborhood and city government, local business organizations, and in the preservation community—local historical societies, historic preservation commissions, and statewide non-profit preservation associations. Preservationists above all strive for a measure of continuity in the built landscape of America's ever-transient human settlements. They seek to enhance the physical evidence of the cultural heritage of humanity, deepening the identity and sense of place of the inhabitants in their natural and built environment. They argue that demolitions of buildings, unless in certifiably dilapidated condition, are acts of violence against our precious natural resources.

Preservation ordinances, initiatives, and advocacy all can reach their aims only through partnerships among institutions and associations that together help communities grow more vital economically and socially. In all these goals, church buildings and the congregations that worship and serve in them are primary elements and constituencies in making preservation work for thriving communities.

Efforts often stumble, though, on issues of money. Who will pay? Who will invest in maintenance and rehabilitation, and what is sufficient economic incentive to attract a conservation-minded developer if a new use is possible? Long-held assumptions about private property kick in again here. Congregations or parishes are assumed to be self-supporting; their members are not accustomed to accepting money from people or organizations outside the membership unless they have some basis of economic exchange such as a lease agreement. Communities assume that a congregation or parish can and should pay its own bills just like a homeowner, a landlord, or a business. Everyone may bemoan that fact that a property is not being kept up, but none would expect to help out with expenses. This is the owner's problem.

Freedom of religious expression ties in neatly with these assumptions. If a group has chosen to erect a building in which to worship and make their presence known in the community, that's entirely their choice and their responsibility. After all, countless other historic properties are under private ownership and the rest of us just have to expect and hope that their owners will keep them up.

As the preservation movement has grown, a number of incentives have been developed to attract owners' investment in upkeep. Tax credits or tax deferrals—federal, state, and local—are available for both income-producing and non-income-producing properties on national or state registers or locally designated as landmarks. But relatively few houses of worship are so designated, and in any case generally do not pay taxes. Tax credits for historic houses of worship are only possible when the congregation has sold the building for another use.

Congregations can apply for grants from public and private sources, but funds are very limited in proportion to the scale of need. Moreover, grants to congregations can become ensnared in First Amendment questions again. Does a grant from a government entity to an actively worshiping congregation constitute the establishment of a particular religion? Some state constitutions are even more explicit than the U.S. constitution, prohibiting the use of public funds for any religious group under any circumstances. Other states have adopted legislation specifically authorizing the use of public funds for protecting historic houses of worship.

Often the courts must try to settle disputes. Is a grant to help stabilize a prominent steeple—a project that requires very expensive foundation work—a contribution to the religious mission of the congregation? What about re-leading and protecting the stained glass windows that many consider a town treasure and premier artistic achievement? In 2018 the New Jersey Supreme Court ruled that the state constitution explicitly bans use of taxes "for building or repairing any church or churches, place or places of worship"—end of story for any public funding of preservation projects. But is it also possible for a court to hold that excluding congregations from public benefits that are available to all other property owners is discriminatory? Is there a distinct and viable line between building needs and religious purposes that would allow a congregation to receive public funds for projects that are externally visible? How are those projects differentiated from work that enhances the congregation's mission?

Of course, private foundations are often also reluctant to make grants for any purpose that might be seen as advancing the mission and activities of a particular religious group. Decisions about whether to give can become complicated for foundations or for individual donors. If I were approached as a non-member to make a charitable contribution to the fund for a new roof on the historic church down the street, would I consider my gift a good way to save the landmark building or an inadvertent means of saving a congregation with whose teachings I sharply disagree?

One solution to these dilemmas is for a congregation to establish a 501.c.3. non-profit corporation that manages funds for building restoration. In that way public or private grants as well as individual donations can be given to an entity like "Historic St. Paul's, Inc." instead of the congregation itself. The funds are under separate management and accounting and legally should not be mingled with church operating funds. Nonetheless, of course, saving the building is still indirectly a help to the congregation and its mission.

The English firebrand historian and journalist Simon Heffer has proposed a way to cut this Gordian knot in the British context, which holds many parallels to the U.S. Declaring himself an atheist, he is also a devotee of England's 12,000 designated historic churches and considers them "a part of what defines me as an Englishman." They are

> one of the major cultural resources of our nation. Is any government, in even the most cash-strapped times, simply going to stand by and watch them crumble?

Heffer argues that the needed upkeep and repairs for Britain's historic churches far exceeds the resources of the Church of England, the counties, or the parishes. Therefore, the historic church buildings should be nationalized and their maintenance as national treasures be included in the national budget. After all, the British monarch as Head of State is the Supreme Governor of the Church; clearly the government must take responsibility for these "great features not just of our landscape and of our life, but of our culture as a people and as a nation."

Heffer's manifesto would raise a hue and cry of protest in the U.S. We have no queen and no national church. The nation was founded in part to be free of such things. Moreover, by far the greatest part of American cultural heritage lies in private hands. We count on private foundations as well as individual or corporate donors to sustain our culture through museums, orchestras, colleges and universities, historic sites, and many other entities. The vast majority of designated historic buildings are privately owned. Any expansion of government into cultural support, such as public television and radio or the National Endowment for the Arts, sparks controversy with those who believe government has no constitutional role in culture.

But that, of course, is hardly the whole picture. Public libraries and schools, national, state, and local parks, museums, and hundreds of historic sites are funded by government for the "general Welfare of the United States" (U.S. Constitution Article I Section 8). Why would it not be possible to fund the maintenance of houses of worship that were designated as national heritage sites, regardless of whatever work the congregation housed there is doing? And couldn't a similar strategy be adopted by states?

This is the kind of radical rethinking and reimagining that will be necessary if America is to save its religious and cultural heritage. Debate over proposals like Heffer's would at the least bring these buildings to the forefront of national consciousness and fire up the passion to save them. A new imagination is also the fuel that drives any approaches to conserving historic houses of worship.

2. Approaches and Scenarios

Here are five approaches described in general; I intend them only as scenarios to spark the imagination and drive the collective will to save and use these buildings. Putting any of these into practice depends on the people, the institutions, the government, and community spirit working together in a local situation. The options are described on a descending scale of desirability with an obvious bias toward the top of this list. Here I provide only a general rationale and perspective for each option; more useful details and case studies are readily available through Partners for Sacred Places and the National Trust for Historic Preservation, as well as many other preservation offices and organizations.

Maintenance and rehabilitation as a building for this congregation collaborating with partner organizations who share the space.

Many congregations give up because they have been overwhelmed by building problems and maintenance tasks. They have concluded that they do not have the money or the human resources to keep pace with building needs. In many cases, congregations will benefit from consulting and training with the "Community Engagement and Asset Mapping" program of Partners for Sacred Places. Here they can learn a whole new approach to their building, much in harmony with asset-based community development (ABCD) methods. A changed perspective enables a congregation to see their building as a community asset instead of an albatross, and to see themselves in partnership with other associations and institutions in the community instead of isolated and self-sufficient. Whatever financial resources they do have become leverage for attracting more support from agencies, foundations, and constituencies beyond the immediate membership.

Many congregations provide social services worth far more to the community than indicated in program budgets. Many provide space for community and group meetings at no charge or for fees far less than comparable commercial rentals. Most churches are homes for the arts—the artistry of craft and décor in the building itself, the practices of music, dance, or visual arts in church and community programs, and the auditory space of sanctuary buildings with acoustics superior to most other sites in town. Many churches, as in North Adams or at Holy Corners, are simply adopted and integrated as part of the public image of a community or a street. In all these ways, congregations with historic buildings are contributing an often-unacknowledged or underestimated economic and social value to the whole community.

Growing numbers of congregations are realizing that their buildings and the programs conducted in them are irreplaceable assets to their wider communities. They need to know how to translate that value into dollars so that a more accurate picture of their contributions can emerge and become leverage for attracting other organizations to share the economic burdens of maintenance. Partners' "Halo Effect" studies provide an effective model for this approach. As congregations develop their case for support and seek capital funding from wider constituencies, they are discovering how wrong their assumption was that nobody outside a congregation cares passionately about the congregation's building—at least not enough to give money. They are learning instead to build partnerships among stakeholders beyond the membership—organizations who lease space in the building, neighborhood groups, local banks, businesses and foundations, neighborhood residents—who want to see the buildings maintained and the programs thrive. Community stakeholders likewise are realizing that they cannot enjoy the steeples as part of the cityscape and appreciate the churches' ministries and spaces while leaving the churches to their own devices for survival. (This is the substance of St. Bartholomew's argument to surrounding neighbors, in the story behind the headline cited at the beginning of this chapter. Shouldn't the mostly high-rise owners and tenants who enjoy the view, the streetscape, and the spaces of this elegantly designed building also help out with maintaining it?)

Many congregations find partners among other worshipping communities—new immigrants who want to share space instead of buying or constructing their own building, or congregations of other faiths, or new congregations whose worship has a different style and constituency from the congregation that owns the building. Shared space must be worked out carefully to avoid unnecessary conflicts, but the payoff comes in the increased energies and synergies of multiple congregations worshipping in the same place.

Congregations, like many owners of historic properties, usually lack the technical expertise to know how best to handle damaged building systems or even to find out what kind of repair is really needed. Through training and consultation with preservation organizations, congregations can learn the benefits of a reliable building conditions assessment and long-term maintenance plan. Such action plans then become a tangible basis for advocating community support of specific needs.

A related possibility is to partner with a rehabilitation architect/builder who already knows and appreciates how to work with historic buildings and their often fragile and tricky materials and designs. In this scenario the builder buys (or leases long-term) and adapts part of the house of worship complex—an education wing, for example—for apartments, condominiums, or offices. Or in a harsher but sometimes necessary scenario, the builder demolishes all or part of a little-used section of the complex and constructs a higher density building on the site—an office or condominium tower, for example. The congregation then uses the new income to complete badly needed maintenance and updates on the worship space as well as other rooms it has retained.

Sale to another congregation or judicatory use for a new congregation

Like most buildings, houses of worship are best used for the purpose for which they were built. Another congregation will make the best buyer and occupant. But the new congregation may be stretched financially to buy the building at all (especially if they are bidding against a developer who has an adaptive use in mind). They may not have the experience or skills they need for proper maintenance or rehabilitation of the building. They may vastly underestimate the challenge they are taking on, especially if they do not have roots in the locale of the building they propose to buy. A congregation that has adopted a previous congregation's house of worship likely will not have the same appreciation for the place and certainly not the stories across generations that made the place itself. This dynamic can easily make a new congregation susceptible to neighborhood redevelopment plans that may include demolition of the building. If the sale is completed, though, and the purchasing congregation wants to serve this particular neighborhood, it needs to consider the strategies discussed in the preceding approach as a way to move forward.

In several church polities when a congregation disbands, the house of worship reverts to a regional judicatory. This opens the possibility of the denomination starting a new congregation in that space, or for a congregation of the same tradition with more resources to open a satellite place of worship there. Maintenance issues remain, of course, but often the spaces of older buildings can be redesigned and rearranged to accommodate the contemporary congregation's needs. Pews can be replaced with movable furniture, brighter lighting can be installed, the platform can be adapted to a more flexible performance space, and many other possibilities. Meanwhile the features that give a historic house of worship its distinct character—plaster arches, stained glass windows, finely crafted wood trim, wainscoting—all can and should be refurbished and preserved as elements attractive particularly in a neighborhood in which people are renovating older homes (or to which people living in apartments or newer suburban homes like to come for a sense of the community's past).

Rehabilitation and reuse for another public purpose

Houses of worship can be adapted for other public activities, as has been proven repeatedly in all regions of the US. Many former church buildings are now performing arts centers, museums, student activities centers for college campuses, libraries, community centers for social services, or public auditoriums—or some combination of these. In each case, the critical element that has been maintained in continuity with the building's history is its nature as a public space.

The significance of this continuing availability of public space cannot be overstated. Many American communities have suffered major losses of places in which people can gather—for performances, speeches, forums, exhibits, classes, receptions, voting, or other public activities. One way the heritage of a building as a house of worship can be sustained into the future is to continue its contribution to a healthy community through its use as a public space. Such use may also help avoid wrangles over zoning, building permits, or business licenses that may ensue from a proposed commercial use.

Rehabilitation and reuse for commercial or residential purposes

The adaptation of houses of worship for offices, stores, or homes results in the privatization of what was a gathering point for at least part of a community. Yet such rehabilitations do preserve the building as a notable element in a historic streetscape. Countless church buildings are now shopping malls, business offices, hotels, restaurants, galleries, studios, condominiums, or single-family homes.

In such adaptations, developers and preservationists should work toward keeping the character-defining elements of the building—such as windows, doors, and towers—intact. For example, many houses of worship feature stained glass windows; occasionally these remain in an adaptive use project but in many cases the historic windows are removed for sale or transfer to other buildings. The design of an adapted building should include some form of window treatment that will not result in large blank areas of glass. Similarly the replacement of wooden doors with full glass doors in metal frames, or the removal of a steeple in favor of a capped square tower, greatly diminishes the historic character of the building.

Demolition of the building with preservation of building elements such as façades for use in other structures

A regrettable but sometimes necessary fifth option for any historic building, the salvage and sale of building elements can only be said to be better than nothing. Preservationists should work to save not only the examples of craft or notable decorations, but also basic building materials such as sills, posts, beams, and roof trusses that cannot be matched or duplicated in new construction. Stained glass windows, carved wooden doors, stone steps or terra cotta pediments, cornices, and window surrounds can find multiple uses in new construction, rehabilitation of other buildings, or creative design of gardens, plazas, or parks.

Nonetheless in full or partial demolition the integrity of the historic building and its contribution to the streetscape of its era is forever lost. Untold thousands of houses of worship have been demolished over the four centuries of modern human settlement in North America. Contemporary society can no longer afford such profligate waste, and the time to find alternatives to demolition is now.

POSTLUDE

Every day across the globe evidence piles up that human beings, particularly in more prosperous "developed" societies, cannot keep living in the way to which we have grown accustomed across the 20th century. As islands of plastic hundreds of miles long drift across the Pacific Ocean, landfills and dumps overflow, centuries-old forests are cut down and their trees are sent to mills for making new furniture or constructing new buildings, carbon emissions increase by the day, and daily internet feeds bring news of disappearing species, we know it is time for change in the way we live and think about the meaning and purpose of life.

Older built landscapes of towns and cities across the nations can contribute to constructive change in two primary ways. First, as the National Trust for Historic Preservation advocates, the greenest building is the building that's already built. The materials are in place, construction energy is invested and embodied in the structure, and natural and aesthetic elements that cannot be replicated make the buildings distinctive and irreplaceable. Second, historic houses of worship and surrounding streetscapes of older buildings typically comprise the highest density districts in a town or city. Here the streets create energy by clustering people and enterprises in a critical mass; this is where "urban buzz" is generated, the crossroads of the town; this is the locus of the synergies, associations, and friendships that create civic and social life. And fossil-fueled transit is much less necessary.

Historic houses of worship offer the public gathering spaces in which those associations can flourish. They will host conflict, too, people at cross-purposes, constituents who have differing pictures of what the neighborhood should be like. They will be places where longtime residents confront newcomers who may represent to them gentrification, rising property values, and higher taxes. They will also be spaces that at least open the possibility of real conversation, of talking through differences, of understanding the points of view of others, and of reaching consensus on how to move forward.

Historic houses of worship have long hosted and sponsored community services, from day care centers to food pantries, from concerts to voting booths, from senior services to homeless shelters. This is a dynamic heritage from which to generate initiatives that serve and build up the community today. This is a base from which to create community partnerships not only to maintain the building but to make it thrive as a center of activity, part of the "glue" of community life.

In the end, historic houses of worship are places of grace. They offer gifts of beauty, extraordinary space, and transcendence that people alive today can only receive from people of the past and do their best to pass them on. They are essential contributors to a generative and creative commons where people can gather and collectively make a life together. They are places of presence. And we are their stewards now.

In der Stadt am Ende der Welt (ink and charcoal on paper 1912): © 2020 Artists Rights Society (ARS), New York / VG Bild-Kunst, Bonn

ENDNOTES BY PAGE NUMBER

Pages xi–xii
> For a brilliant analysis of nostalgia and its effects, see Svetlana Boym, *The Future of Nostalgia* (New York: Basic Books, 2001).

Page 2
> R. Stephen Warner, "The Place of the Congregation in the American Religious Configuration," in *New Perspectives in the Study of Congregations: American Congregations* Vol. 2, ed. by James P. Wind and James W. Lewis (Chicago: University of Chicago Press, 1994) 54–99.

Pages 4–7
> For a broad-ranging study of contemporary trends in American congregations including membership data, see Mark Chaves, *Congregations in America* (Cambridge: Harvard University Press, 2004) and his more recent study *American Religion: Contemporary Trends* (Princeton: Princeton University Press, 2011).

> For an overview of factors in the nationwide diminishing of older Protestant denominations, see Thomas

Edward Frank, *Polity, Practice, and the Mission of The United Methodist Church* (Nashville: Abingdon Press, 1997, 2006) Chapter 2.

Pages 11–12

Joe Manning, *Steeples: Sketches of North Adams* and *Disappearing into North Adams* (Florence, MA: Flatiron Press, 2001). See also Joe Manning's website, www.morningsonmaplestreet.com.

Page 13

The story of St. John's United Methodist Church has been compiled from historical accounts photocopied for the church's Centennial Celebration (2001–2003); "The Churches of St. Louis" series published in *The Spectator* II (84) April 22, 1882: 581; a photocopy of a 1940s Year Book of the church written by Ivan Lee Holt, its longtime pastor and later a Methodist bishop; and the "Nineteenth Century Church Survey of St. Louis" (photocopy), compiled by the Landmarks Association of St. Louis, Inc.

Pages 16–17

Neola McCorkle Koechig, *The Story of Second Baptist Church of Greater St. Louis* (published by the church, 1982).

Samuel Rosenkrantz, Ed., A Centennial History of Congregation Temple Israel 1886–1986 5647–5747 (Creve Coeur, MO: Congregation Temple Israel, 1986).

Page 18

Urban renewal in St. Louis has been explored through numerous articles and websites; see for example the work by Colin Gordon at http://mappingdecline.lib.uiowa.edu/map/ and his book *Mapping Decline: St. Louis and the Fate of the American City* (Philadelphia: University of Pennsylvania Press, 2009); and Ryan DeLoach and Jenn DeRose at

http://www.decodingstl.org/urban-renewal-and-mill-creek-valley/

Pages 19, 21

Colin Gordon's website also tracks the real estate and zoning strategy to keep African Americans and "whites" in separate neighborhoods north and south of Delmar Boulevard: http://mappingdecline.lib.uiowa.edu/map/

Page 23

The City of St. Louis designated historic landmarks list may be found at:

https://www.stlouis-mo.gov/government/departments/planning/cultural-resources/city-landmarks/

Page 26

Pierre Nora, *Les Lieux de Mémoire* (Editions Gallimard, 1992); English translation, revised and abridged edition published as *Realms of Memory*, 3 Vols. (New York: Columbia University Press, 1997); see especially Vol. 2, *The Construction of the French Past*.

Page 27

Gwen W. Steege, "The 'Book of Plans' and the Early Romanesque Revival in the United States: A Study in Architectural Patronage" *Journal of the Society of Architectural Historians* 46:3 (September 1987) 215–227. Quote on steeples is found on p. 219; the article also discusses the plan book published by the Congregational Church denomination in 1853.

Pages 28–29

Thomas A. Griffin, "Historical Discourse: Origin and Progress of Methodism in North Adams" [delivered at the closing of the old building, April 21, 1872] (North Adams: James T. Robinson and Son Printers, 1872) 24. Other historical information may be found in booklets held by the North Adams Public Library archives: "First Methodist Episcopal Church, North Adams, Massachusetts, 1873–1927" and "First Methodist Episcopal Church, North Adams, Massachusetts, Program of Dedication" [1929].

Page 31

On congregational memory, see Jennifer Clark, "'This Special Shell': The Church Building and the Embodiment of Memory" *The Journal of Religious History* 31:1 (March 2007) 59–77.

See also Thomas Edward Frank, *The Soul of the Congregation: An Invitation to Congregational Reflection* (Nashville: Abingdon Press, 2000) 90–91.

Danièle Hervieu-Léger, *Religion as a Chain of Memory* (London: Polity Press, 2000); see especially Chapter 7, "Religion Deprived of Memory." Quotes may be found in the discussion on pp. 123–33.

Page 41

Michael Hoberman, "High Crimes and Fallen Factories: Nostalgic Utopianism in an Eclipsed New England Industrial Town" *Oral History Review* 28:1 (Winter/Spring 2001) 17–40.

Page 43

Maurice Halbwachs, *La Mémoire Collective* (1950), translated into English as *The Collective Memory* (New York: Harper and Row Colophon Books, 1980).

Page 48
> Wallace Stegner, "The Sense of Place" in *Where the Bluebird Sings to the Lemonade Springs: Living and Writing in the West* (New York: Penguin Books, 1992) 199–206.

Page 49
> Joe Manning, *Disappearing into North Adams*, 192, 297.

Pages 50–51
> *Addresses and Papers Presented at the Diamond Jubilee 1827–1902, May 11–14 1902* First Congregational Church, North Adams, Massachusetts (North Adams: The Advance Press, 1902).
>
> Dorothy (Stockwell) Amato, *A History of St. John's Church, North Adams, Massachusetts, 1855–1996* (n.d., published by St. John's Church).

Page 52
> Christopher Alexander, *A Pattern Language: Towns, Buildings, Construction* (New York: Oxford University Press, 1977).

Pages 53–54
> András Roman, "Intangibility in Historic Towns," unpublished paper delivered at the 14th General Assembly and International Symposium, International Council on Monuments and Sites (ICOMOS) (2003). Roman was founding president of the ICOMOS International Committee of Historic Towns and Villages.
>
> Joao Campos, "The Wise Use of Heritage," abstracts from the World Congress of the Conservation of Cultural Heritage, ICOMOS, 1999.
>
> Both papers available online at https://www.icomos.org/en in Open Archive.

Pages 54–55

Manning, *Disappearing*, 302.

Page 57

Denis Cosgrove, "Geography is Everywhere: Culture and Symbolism in Human Landscapes" reprinted from *Horizons in Human Geography* (1988) in *The Cultural Geography Reader*, ed. by Timothy S. Oakes and Patricia L. Price (London: Routledge, 2008) 176–185.

Page 58

Frederick Rudolph, "Chinamen in Yankeedom: Anti-Unionism in Massachusetts in 1870" *The American Historical Review* 53, no. 1 (1947): 1–29.

Pages 60–61

The "Sustainable Berkshires" report including a section on Historic Preservation may be found at http://berkshireplanning.org/reports-and-documents.

Page 65

Peter W. Williams, "Sacred Space in North America" *Journal of the American Academy of Religion* 70:3 (September 2002) 593–609. Williams reviewed five books, including David Chidester and Edward Linenthal, eds., *American Sacred Space* (Bloomington: Indiana University Press, 1995).

Pages 70–71

Boston Globe (December 29, 2003) A10.

Parish data from the Berkshires published in *Catholic Mirror* (May/June 2018) 20–21.

Pages 72–73

The term "civic" churches appeared in David A. Roozen, William McKinney, and Jackson W. Carroll,

Varieties of Religious Presence: Mission in Public Life (New York: Pilgrim Press, 1984).

Chidester and Linenthal, *American Sacred Space*, Introduction, 8.

Page 78

A summary of Partners for Sacred Places' study of the Halo Effect may be downloaded at http://sacredplaces.org/uploads/files/16879092466251061-economic-halo-effect-of-historic-sacred-places.pdf.

Pages 81–82

An extensive planning vision for North Adams created by Thomas Krens was covered by the *New York Times* Real Estate section (April 15, 2018) 8.

Pages 86–87

Julio Bermudez, Ed., *Transcending Architecture: Contemporary Views on Sacred Space* (Washington, D.C.: Catholic University of America Press, 2015).

Chidester and Linenthal, *American Sacred Space*, Introduction, 5–6.

Page 88

Pierre Bourdieu, *Outline of a Theory of Practice* (New York: Cambridge University Press, 1977) 81.

Pages 89–90

New York Times Design section (May 10, 2018) 20–21.

Pages 90–91

Lindsay Jones, *The Hermeneutics of Sacred Architecture: Experience, Interpretation, Comparison* Vol I, *Monumental Occasions: Reflections on the Eventfulness of Religious Architecture* (Cambridge: Harvard University Press, 2000) 144, 200 ff.

Page 95

Anne Buttimer, "Home, Reach, and the Sense of Place" in Anne Buttimer and David Seaman, eds., *The Human Experience of Space and Place* (New York: St. Martin's Press, 1980) 170–172.

Page 98

Richard Kieckhefer, *Theology in Stone: Church Architecture from Byzantium to Berkeley* (Oxford: Oxford University Press, 2004) Chapters 1–4.

Pages 100–101

See the website for Link Auction Galleries, Inc., which has a photo of the building as well as staff photos posed in front of the fluted columns. There are no photos of the display rooms probably for security reasons.

Pages 102–103

For more on Grace Restaurant, now an events space, see https://www.trineeventsgrace.com/. I am also grateful to my friend Valerie Wyman for sharing her memories of this building as Chestnut Street Methodist Church—her wedding there, and her father's ministry in the Portland area.

Page 107

Thomas F. Pike, *Preservation Forum* 1:2 Winter 1987–88, pp. 6–8.

Pages 107–109

A useful summary of court cases involving historic houses of worship may be found in Norman Tyler,

Ilene R. Tyler, and Ted J. Ligibel, *Historic Preservation: An Introduction to Its History, Principles, and Practice*, Third Edition (New York: W. W. Norton and Company, 2009, 2018) Chapter 4.

On Springfield, MA, see:

http://www.masslive.com/news/index.ssf/2013/07/us_court_of_appeals_upholds_hi.html

http://www.masslive.com/news/index.ssf/2016/05/stained_glass_windows_at_sprin.html

On Cleveland, OH, see:

http://www.cleveland.com/business/index.ssf/2013/11/cleveland_landmarks_commission_2.html

Page 115

On the New Jersey court case, see *New York Times* (April 25, 2018) A20.

Page 117

Simon Heffer, "Why Churches Matter" posted in the National Churches Trust website under the tab "Discover Churches": https://www.nationalchurchestrust.org/discover-churches/why-churches-matter.

Old North Church in Boston exemplifies the power of national landmark designation for religious sites that represent critical moments in American history, which places them under the protection of the National Park Service; see https://www.nps.gov/bost/learn/historyculture/onc.htm.

Page 119

For more information on "Community Engagement and Asset Mapping" consulting and training programs of Partners for Sacred Places, see https://

sacredplaces.org/reimagine-your-sacred-place/consulting-services/#Community%20Engagement%20&%20Asset%20Mapping.

Pages 127–128

Stephanie A. Meeks with Kevin C. Murphy, *The Past and Future City: How Historic Preservation is Reviving America's Communities* (Washington, D.C.: National Trust for Historic Preservation, 2016). See especially Chapter 2, "Older, Smaller, Better: How Older Buildings Enhance Urban Vitality" and Chapter 7, "The Greenest Buildings: Preservation, Climate Change, and the Environment." The National Trust re-urbanism and green initiatives may be found under: https://savingplaces.org/reurbanism#.XWQxSuhKg2w.

APPENDIX: WHERE TO BEGIN

*Resources for
Congregations and Communities*

Partners for Sacred Places (sacredplaces.org)

A national, non-sectarian, non-profit headquartered in Philadelphia, Partners offers a wide range of resources from consulting to published studies to training programs and more. Partners is the place to start when a congregation is beginning to explore the future of its historic building.

National Trust for Historic Preservation
(savingplaces.org)

The National Trust is the indispensable collaborator with Partners in the National Fund for Sacred Places, which is able to assist selected applicants with seed money for capital funds campaigns. These houses of worship, from all over the United States, located in varied settings, and representing diverse religious traditions, then become exemplars of what can be done and an inspiration to others.

The Trust also collects its own stories and resources on the rehabilitation and revitalization of houses of worship and their surrounding neighborhoods. These and other resources may be found on the website at: https://savingplaces.org/sacred-places-theme#.XWf2_ChKg2w

State Historic Preservation Offices (national directory may be found at http://ncshpo.org/directory/)

Popularly known as SHPO's, these offices are located at the capitol of each state or territory of the U.S. and are funded through a collaboration of federal and state government. They are the chief administrators of the National Historic Preservation Act of 1966. They oversee tax credit programs, provide resources for rehabilitation, and support historic preservation commissions in local places such as cities or counties. The process for nominating a historic property for the National Register of Historic Places begins in this office.

Statewide non-profit preservation organizations

Most states have a preservation association that offers resources for the whole state. Some are quite well-developed and feature information, annual conferences, and case studies helpful for conserving houses of worship. Preservation North Carolina is among those that provide a list of all such organizations: https://www.presnc.org/state-nonprofit-preservation-organizations/

Another website that collects myriad links to state and local historical societies and preservation organizations may be found here: https://www.preservationdirectory.com/preservationorganizationsresources/organizationcategories.aspx

Local historic preservation commissions and nonprofit associations are also a good place to start making connections with resources. Such offices can help network congregations that face similar issues, and assist congregations in developing a healthy relationship with the local historic district in which they may be located.

The Main Street America program (https://www.mainstreet.org/home) is a good place for congregations and communities to start imagining and planning for ways to collaborate in revitalizing neighborhoods. These initiatives usually involve local government such as planning departments and town or city council members, as well as public school systems, parks and recreation, neighborhood associations, and major businesses such as banks and retail stores. Unified approaches to creating healthy neighborhoods put the preservation challenges of a historic house of worship in a larger context of bringing new life to historic neighborhoods.

Non-profit organizations compiling information on houses of worship of a particular heritage, ethnicity, or region

Historic Rural Churches of Georgia (https://www.hrcga.org/) is a relatively new organization that has been collecting photographs and stories of rural and often remote houses of worship across the Georgia countryside, and has produced a handsome book to help bring public attention to these treasures. Other states such as Minnesota have published similar books as well as survey studies, either through the statewide preservation association, the state historical society, or the State Historic Preservation Office.

Religious heritages or denominations also keep some records of historic houses of worship and offer resources for study that can be useful for particular local congregations as well as larger regions. The United Methodist Church process of designating landmarks, for example, may be found here: http://gcah.org/resources/heritage-landmarks. A Roman Catholic historic travel guide for the U.S. may be found here: https://thecatholictravelguide.com/destinations/u-s-a/. Photos and stories of synagogues may be found in a variety of books and websites such as the American Jewish Historical Society (http://www.ajhs.org/rediscovering-jewish-infrastructure-table). The online historical resources center BlackPast has posted a list of historic African American churches at https://www.blackpast.org/special-features/historic-african-american-churches/.

These initiatives play a vital role in keeping historic houses of worship in the forefront of public awareness. What is often more difficult to find, however, is resources provided by a heritage or denomination that are directly related to conserving buildings and finding new community partners and collaborations. This is where the Partners organization and website and others listed above become so useful.

ACKNOWLEDGMENTS

This book has been in formation for nearly 14 years. All along the way I have enjoyed both institutional and personal support that has kept me going and renewed my passion for historic houses of worship and their future. The manuscript now becomes a book through the support of Library Partners Press and particularly Bill Kane, friend and Wake Forest colleague in many blue-sky ideations that he so often brings to creative and innovative reality.

The seed of this book was planted when I first connected with Partners for Sacred Places, a national non-profit with headquarters in Philadelphia. Over these years President Bob Jaeger has become a colleague, friend, and inspiration. Tuomi Forrest, long-time staff member and now executive director of Historic Germantown (PA), engaged with me in many wide-ranging conversations about the complex issues and promising possibilities associated with these buildings. I thank him especially for reading the manuscript and as usual offering many useful comments. Sarah Peveler, now retired, was my initial contact with the Partners asset-based approach to transforming congregations' attitudes about their properties and communities. Together we explored many different possible ways to connect congregations in historic buildings with each other and with future leaders in training through theological education.

My years chairing the Partners Board of Directors (2006–2011) were immensely fruitful for me. The Board members have always been a diverse group, bringing varied experiences and ideas to bear not only on Partners' organization but also on the challenges facing houses of worship generally. Those years of economic downturn were difficult for all non-profits, and I was not the only one who thought the whole enterprise of coordinated efforts to save and revitalize historic churches and synagogues was at risk. Yet again, the seeds of ideas such as a National Fund for Sacred Places were planted then and as the economy strengthened have now come to fruition through a collaboration of Partners and the National Trust for Historic Preservation. All along the way, the Lilly Endowment, Inc., and its staff leadership of Craig Dykstra, Chris Coble, and especially John Wimmer, have offered indispensable support.

Immediately before becoming chair of the Partners board, I completed a master's degree in Heritage Preservation at Georgia State University. The leaders of this path-breaking degree program, Tim Crimmins and Richard Laub, were not only key teachers and guides for me in learning the field, but also most helpful in getting me started on promising directions for research. At that same time, the then State Historic Preservation Officer for Georgia, Ray Luce, became my supervisor for an internship and assisted in my project of creating a potential state resource for historic houses of worship—a keen interest we shared.

This book and its case studies occupied much of my last decade of teaching at Emory University. I am grateful to the Candler School of Theology for a continuous stream of small research grants, and to my colleagues who read and commented as usual with uncommon insight on the earliest versions of this manuscript. During that same period I presented some of this material at sessions of both the American Academy of Religion and the Religious Research Association, and am grateful for the many useful comments from colleagues in those settings as well.

In this most recent decade at Wake Forest University I have gained greatly from my collegiality and mutual support of research projects with faculty of the Department of History and the School of Divinity. I learned much from the opportunity to present this material at the interdisciplinary Social Sciences Research Seminar.

Case studies have always been the critical center of this project and I am deeply grateful to the many people both in North Adams and in St. Louis who have provided crucial information and contacts in support of this work. Justyna Carlson and her husband Gene know much of what needs to be known about North Adams. Both are immersed in preservation activities, Justyna through her leadership in the local Historical Commission and in the religious community, and Gene through his avid volunteering with the North Adams Historical Museum. I am thankful for their unfailing flow of news, updates, and insights, and also for their friendship. Justyna read the manuscript and offered many helpful corrections and comments. I express my appreciation to the many North Adams residents who agreed to be interviewed, particularly Mayors John Barrett and Richard Alcombright, as well as other accomplished city staff members. I interviewed a number of church leaders and owners of houses of worship now used for new purposes and appreciate their enthusiastic cooperation. The libraries and staffs of the North Adams Public Library and the Freel Library of Massachusetts College of Liberal Arts were most helpful and a treasure trove of historic documents and photographs.

As always, my guide and fellow fanatic in the exploration of urban landscapes, Martin Braeske, helped me with news and connections in St. Louis where I have not lived for a long time. Our shared obsessions have grown into an abiding friendship over many years. My colleague and friend Ken Gottman, who himself serves as pastor in a historic house of worship, has always followed my project and my work with Partners, and even made a site visit on my behalf. I found many materials cited in this book in the Missouri Historical Society archives and in the records of the Landmarks Association of St. Louis.

Acknowledgments

My extended family and community of friends have often asked me how this project is going, and resisted rolling their eyes upon hearing that I was still working on the manuscript. But no one writing a book can bring it to completion without that kind of love and support. I am especially grateful to my sister Susan Frank Parsons and her husband Mark Parsons, principal of Parsons Sargeant Architects who work extensively with historic churches in England, for their reading and commenting on the manuscript.

Which brings me above all to Gail O'Day, my wife, my soulmate over most of my adult life, who got me hooked on North Adams, discussed my ideas, joined me on research trips, and listened to my endless reports and analysis for over a decade. I miss her immeasurably even as her presence in my life remains, and I dedicate this book to the memory of her remarkable life.

www.ingramcontent.com/pod-product-compliance
Lightning Source LLC
Chambersburg PA
CBHW071459150426
43191CB00008B/1391